George Sowerby

Marine shells of South Africa

A catalogue of all the known species

George Sowerby

Marine shells of South Africa
A catalogue of all the known species

ISBN/EAN: 9783337124595

Printed in Europe, USA, Canada, Australia, Japan

Cover: Foto ©Andreas Hilbeck / pixelio.de

More available books at **www.hansebooks.com**

MARINE SHELLS

OF

SOUTH AFRICA

A CATALOGUE OF ALL THE KNOWN SPECIES

WITH

REFERENCES TO FIGURES IN VARIOUS WORKS, DESCRIPTIONS
OF NEW SPECIES, AND FIGURES OF SUCH AS ARE NEW,
LITTLE KNOWN, OR HITHERTO UNFIGURED

BY

G. B. SOWERBY, F.L.S., F.Z.S.

LONDON
SOWERBY, 121 FULHAM ROAD, S.W.
1892

PRINTED BY

AND CO., NEW STREET SQUARE

LONDON

PREFACE.

RECEIVING some years ago a quantity of shells from Port
Elizabeth, some of which I could not identify with any that
had been described, I contributed a paper to the 'Journal of
Conchology,' January 1886, consisting of a list of those I had
identified, and descriptions of those which appeared to be
new. This led to the publication of two subsequent papers
in the same Journal, through my communications to the
Conchological Society in 1889, considerably increasing the
list. Since then, various friends in South Africa have
discovered many additional species, some of which are well-
known inhabitants of other coasts, but not previously recorded
as South African.

The purpose of the present work is to give in a small
compass a list, as complete as possible, of all the known
Marine Shells of South Africa, with references to figures in
well-known works, descriptions of new species, and figures
not only of these, but of some that have been described
from time to time by other authors without figures.

The total number of species enumerated is 740. Of
these, 67 are also found in European seas, 340 are known
to inhabit other coasts, and the remaining 323 are, as far as
is known, confined to South Africa.

The labour of sorting and identifying so many species
(many of them very minute) has been considerable, and the

completeness with which I have have been enabled to accom-
plish the task has been due to a great extent to the zeal of
John H. Ponsonby, Esq., through whom I have received a large
proportion of the material, and to the kindly and courteous
aid rendered to me by Edgar A. Smith, Esq., of the Zoological
Department, British Museum.   Lastly, I have had the
advantage of thoroughly examining the collection formed at
Port Elizabeth by S. D. Bairstow, Esq., F.L.S., recently
presented by him to the Oxford University Museum, which
contains a fair proportion of my types.

   The present Catalogue may be regarded as a supplement
to the excellent work of Dr. Ferdinand Krauss published in
1848.

   It will be observed that some of the generic names are
not the same as those in common use, and differ from those
in the 'Thesaurus Conchyliorum,' 'Conchologia Iconica,'
and other standard works.   These names I am compelled to
adopt by the inexorable law of priority, but the following
list will render them intelligible :—

   Actæon, *Montfort*, 1810 = *Tornatella* (Lamk. 1812).
   Ancilla, *Lamarck*, 1799 = *Ancillaria* (Lamk. 1811).
   Calliostoma, *Bruguière*, 1840 = *Ziziphinus* (Gray, 1840).
   Cuspidaria, *Nardo*, 1840 = *Neæra* (Gray, non Rob.-Dev.).
   Dosinia, *Scopoli*, 1777 = *Artemis* (Poli, 1791).
   Gastrana, *Schumacher*, 1817 = *Diodonta* (Desh. 1846).
   Ovula, *Bruguière*, 1789 = *Ovulum* (Sowerby &c.).
   Oxynoë, *Rafinesque*, 1819 = *Lophocercus* (Krohn, 1847).
   Scutum, *Montfort*, 1810 = *Parmophorus* (Blv. 1817).
   Sistrum, *Montfort*, 1810 = *Ricinula* (Lamk. 1812).
   Turbonilla, *Leach*, 1826 = *Chemnitzia* (D'Orb. 1829).

MARINE SHELLS

OF

SOUTH AFRICA.

CEPHALOPODA.

ARGONAUTA ARGO, *Linn.*—Frequently found on the shores of South Africa; also in the Atlantic, Pacific, and Mediterranean.

ARGONAUTA BÖTTGERI, *Maltzan*, Journ. de Conch. vol. xxix. p. 163, pl. 6, fig. 7. See Journal of Conchology, vol. vi. 1889.—South Africa, Mauritius, China, &c.

SPIRULA PERONI, *Lamarck.* Of world-wide distribution. —Port Elizabeth (occasionally found on the beach).

PTEROPODA.

HYALÆA TRIDENTATA, *Forskael.* This well-known species, abundant in the Atlantic and Mediterranean, is occasionally found in South African waters.

HYALÆA TRUNCATA, *Krauss*, Sudafr. Moll. p. 34, pl. 2, fig. 12.—I am not acquainted with this shell, but have considerable doubt as to its being distinct from *H. tridentata.*

HYALÆA LIMBATA, *D'Orbigny.*—A well-known species, abundant in the Atlantic. A few specimens have been found at Port Elizabeth.

B

HYALÆA GLOBULOSA, *Rang.*—Common in the Atlantic and Pacific Oceans. Occasionally found on the South African coasts.

STYLIOLA RECTA, *Lesueur = Creseis aciculata* (D'Orbigny), Sowb. in Conch. Icon. Pteropoda, pl. 5, fig. 29.—Port Elizabeth, &c.

GASTROPODA.

MUREX BREVISPINA, *Lamarck*, Conch. Icon. (Murex), pl. 19, fig. 77, *Krauss*, Sudafr. Moll. p. 111.—Natal Bay.

MUREX (OCINEBRA?) PURPUROIDES, *Dunker, Reeve*, Conch. Icon. pl. 32, fig. 153 = *M. Dunkeri* (Krauss), Sudafr. Moll. p. 112, tab. vi. fig. 14.—Port Elizabeth, Cape, and Natal coasts.

MUREX (OCINEBRA?) SCROBICULATUS, *Dunker* (Fusus), Philippi, Abbild. vol. ii. p. 12, pl. 3, fig. 4.—This species being perfectly distinct from *M. purpuroides*, has been commonly but erroneously taken for *M. Dunkeri* (Krauss), which is simply a synonym for *M. purpuroides.* — Port Elizabeth, &c.

MUREX (OCINEBRA?) KIENERI, *Reeve*, Conch. Icon. sp. 172. —Algoa Bay and Natal coast.

MUREX (OCINEBRA?) CRAWFORDI, *Sowerby*, nov. sp. (plate 1, fig. 2).—Testa subventricosa, solidiuscula, straminea; spira acuminata, sutura canaliculata; anfractus 5½, convexi, rotundati, liris numerosis elevatis subnodulosis spiraliter cingulati; anfractus ultimus inflatus, rotundatus, inferne haud productus; apertura ovata, columella levissime arcuata, glabra, truncata, canali brevissimo; labrum crenulatum.

Long. 12, lat. maj. 7 millim.

This species is closely allied to *M. scrobiculatus*, but differs constantly in its shorter form, and the absence of a rostrum, the base of the columella being abruptly truncated. It may also be distinguished by the presence of an additional rib on the penultimate whorl.

MUREX (OCINEBRA?) BABINGTONI, *Sowerby*, nov. sp. pl. 1, fig. 1.—Testa fusiformis. luteo-fusca ; spira elongata,

turrita; sutura canaliculata ; anfractus 6½, convexi, rotundati
aut angulati; liris numerosis elevatis submodulosis spiraliter
cingulati, longitudinaliter interplicati ; anfr. ultimus sub-
inflatus, rotundatus, inferne rostratus; rostrum subelongatum,
leviter recurvum ; apertura ovata; peristoma simplex; columella levissime arcuata, glabra ; canalis longiusculus.

Long. 15, diam. maj. 8 ; apert. longa 5, lata 3 millim.

Hab. Port Elizabeth.

This species is similar in sculpture to *M. scrobiculatus*,
from which it differs considerably in form, the spire being
long and turreted, and the rostrum elongated and slightly
recurved. In form the shell is somewhat similar to the
British *Trophon muricatus*, and would have appeared to
belong rather to the genus *Trophon* than to *Murex*, but
that it has evident affinity with the four last-named species,
which appear to belong to the genus or sub-genus *Ocinebra*,
or perhaps it may be found, when the animals are known,
that these five species form a separate group.

MUREX (POROPTERON) MITRÆFORMIS, *Sowerby*, Conch.
Illust. fig. 75.—Cape, and Natal coast. Rare.

MUREX (POROPTERON) UNCINARIUS, *Lamarck*=*M. capensis* (Sowerby), Conch. Illust. fig. 76.—Rather common
at Port Elizabeth.

TROPHON WAHLBERGI, *Krauss* (Murex), Sudafr. Moll.
p. 111, pl. 6, fig. 13.—Natal coast (Krauss).

TYPHIS ARCUATUS, *Hinds*, Proc. Zool. Soc. 1843, p. 19 :
Zool. Voy. Sulphur, Moll. p. 10, pl. 4, f. 1, 2.—Agulhas
Bank, 40-45 fath. (Hinds).

FUSUS ROBUSTIOR, *Sowerby*, Thes. Conch. vol. iv. p. 82,
fig. 63.—Port Elizabeth.

FUSUS RUBRO-LINEATUS, *Sowerby*, Proc. Zool. Soc. 1870,
p. 252 ; Thes. Conch. vol. iv. p. 80, pl. 411, fig. 68.—Agulhas
Bank (Denicke).

FUSUS CLAUSICAUDATUS, *Hinds*, Zool. Voy. Sulphur,
Moll. p. 13, pl. I, fig. 10, 11, Sowerby, Thes. Conch. vol. iv.
fig. 55.—Agulhas Bank (Hinds). This remarkable shell, now
in the British Museum, is believed to be unique.

SIPHONALIA MANDARINA, *Duclos* (Fusus), Mag. de Zool. 1831, pl. 8; Sowerby, Thes. Conch. pl. 7, fig. 71.—Natal coast (Krauss). This species is found on the coast of New Zealand. I have not met with it among South African shells.

EUTHRIA WAHLBERGI, *Krauss* (Purpura), Sudafr. Moll. p. 118, pl. 6, fig. 15; Smith, P. Z. S., 1891, p. 435, pl. 4, fig. 2, as *Coralliophila*.—Natal coast (Krauss).

EUTHRIA LINEOLATA, *Dunker* (Fusus), Philippi, Abbild. 110, pl. 1, fig. 10.—Port Elizabeth.

EUTHRIA FUSCO-TINCTA, Sowerby, pl. 1, fig. 13; Journ. of Conch. vol. v. p. 4; vol. vi. pl. 1, fig. 18.—Port Elizabeth.

EUTHRIA PONSONBYI, *Sowerby*, pl. 1, fig. 12; Journ. of Conch. vol. vi. p. 149.—Port Elizabeth.

EUTHRIA SIMONIANA, *Petit*, Journ. de Conch. vol. iii. pl. 7, fig. 7.—Cape of Good Hope (Petit).

TRITONIDEA RUBIGINOSA, *Reeve* (Buccinum), Conch. Icon. pl. 7, fig. 47, *var. scabricostata*; Krauss, Sudafr. Moll. p. 120.—Natal coast (Krauss).

TRITONIDEA UNDOSA, var. *minor*, *Sowerby*, Journ. of Conch. vol. vi. p. 148.—Port Elizabeth.

PYRULA PARADISIACA, *Reeve*, Conch. Icon. pl. v. fig. 17b, —Port Elizabeth (rare). Common in the Red Sea, &c.

METULA MARMORATA, *Reeve* (Buccinum), Conch. Icon. pl. 12, fig. 95.—Port Elizabeth (rare). Common on the coast of Mauritius.

PLEUROTOMA (?) FULGURANS, *Krauss*, Sudafr. Moll. p. 109, pl. 6, fig. 11.—This shell is unknown to me, but from figure and description I have considerable doubt as to its belonging to the *Pleurotomidæ*.

PLEUROTOMA (DRILLIA) WILKLÆ, *Sowerby*, pl. 1, fig. 4; Journ. of Conch. vol. vi. 1889, p. 7, pl. 1, fig. 21.—Port Elizabeth.

PLEUROTOMA (DRILLIA) GRAYI, *Reeve*, Proc. Zool. Soc. 1845, p. 114; Conch. Icon. sp. 232; Sowerby, Journ. of Conch. 1889, vol. vi. p. 149.—I have lately received several perfect specimens of this species. They are darker in colour than the worn shell mentioned in my paper of 1889, and have a narrow whitish band below the middle of the body whorl.

PLEUROTOMA (DRILLIA) PLATYSTOMA, *Smith*, plate 4, fig. 82; Ann. and Mag. Nat. Hist. 1877, vol. xix. p. 501.—Port Elizabeth.

PLEUROTOMA (DRILLIA) FULTONI, *Sowerby*, Proc. Zool. Soc. 1888, p. 210, pl. xi. f. 17; Journ. of Conch. vol. vi. 1889. —Port Elizabeth.

PLEUROTOMA (DRILLIA) CASTANEA, *Reeve*, Conch. Icon. sp. 191; Sowb. Journ. of Conch. vol. v. 1886, p. 7.—Port Elizabeth.

PLEUROTOMA (CLAVUS) HOTTENTOTA, *Smith*, pl. 4, fig. 81; Ann. and Mag. of Nat. Hist. 1882, vol. x. p. 208.—Port Elizabeth.

PLEUROTOMA (CLAVUS?) NUX, *Reeve*, Ann. and Mag. of Nat. Hist. 1846, p. 364; Reeve, Conch. Icon. pl. 21, fig. 185.—Cape of Good Hope (Reeve).

PLEUROTOMA (CLAVUS) FUCATA, *Reeve*, Conch. Icon. sp. 169.—Port Elizabeth (rare).

PLEUROTOMA (CLAVATULA) GRAVIS, *Hinds*, Proc. Zool. Soc. 1843, p. 37; Zool. Voy. Sulphur, Moll. p. 16, pl. 5, fig. 8.— Agulhas Bank.

PLEUROTOMA (CLAVATULA) RUBINICOLOR, *Reeve*, Conch. Icon. sp. 184.—Cape coast.

PLEUROTOMA (CLAVATULA) STOLIDA, *Hinds*, Reeve, Conch. Icon. sp. 152.—Agulhas Bank.

PLEUROTOMA (CLAVATULA) TAXUS, *Chemnitz*, Reeve, Conch. Icon. f. 25.—This fine species is certainly South African, but my friends have not yet been able to procure specimens.

PLEUROTOMA (CLAVATULA) TUMIDA, *Sowerby*, Proc. Zool. Soc. 1870, p. 253.—A single specimen, now in the British Museum, was dredged by Captain Denicke at Agulhas Bank.

PLEUROTOMA (CRASSISPIRA) ROUSI, *Sowerby*, pl. 1, fig. 3; Journ. of Conch. vol. v. Jan. 1886.

PLEUROTOMA (CLIONELLA) SINUATA, *Born* = *P. buccinoides*, Kiener, p. 38, pl. 13, fig. 1; Reeve, Conch.

Icon. fig. 68.—This species is peculiar to South Africa. It varies very much in the prominence of the longitudinal ribs, which in some specimens are obsolete.

PLEUROTOMA (CLIONELLA) SEMICOSTATA, *Kiener*, Icon. Coq. Viv. p. 39, pl. 19, fig. 1.—Cape coast (Krauss).

PLEUROTOMA (CLIONELLA) ROSARIA, *Reeve*, Conch. Icon. sp. 311.—I doubt very much whether this can be properly separated from the extremely variable *P. sinuata*.

PLEUROTOMA (CLIONELLA) BAIRSTOWI, *Sowerby*, pl. 1, fig. 6 ; Journ. of Conch. vol. v. p. 8.—Port Elizabeth.

PLEUROTOMA (CLIONELLA) BORNII, *E. A. Smith*, pl. 4, fig. 77 ; Ann. and Mag. of Nat. Hist. 1877, vol. xix. p. 499.—Cape of Good Hope.

PLEUROTOMA (CLIONELLA) TRIPARTITA, *E. A. Smith*, pl. 4, fig. 83 ; Weinkauff, Conch. Cab. ed. 2, 120, pl. 26. figs. 12 and 13.—Tyron thought this to be *P. obesa* (Reeve), but it is quite unlike it, and certainly belongs to a different section of the genus.

PLEUROTOMA (CLIONELLA) SUBVENTRICOSA, *E. A. Smith*, pl. 4, fig. 76 ; Ann. and Mag. of Nat. Hist. 1877, vol. xix. p. 500.—Various South African localities.

PLEUROTOMA (CLIONELLA) SIGILLATA, *Reeve*, Conch. Icon. sp. 363.—Cape of Good Hope (Reeve).

PLEUROTOMA (CLIONELLA) DIVERSA, *E. A. Smith*, pl. 4, fig. 79 ; Ann. and Mag. of Nat. Hist. 1882, vol. x. p. 207.—Port Elizabeth.

PLEUROTOMA (CLIONELLA) CAFFRA, *E. A. Smith*, pl. 4, fig. 80 ; Ann. and Mag. of Nat. Hist. 1882, vol. x. p. 209.—Port Elizabeth.

PLEUROTOMA (CLIONELLA) KRAUSSII, *E. A. Smith*, pl. 4, fig. 78 ; Ann. and Mag. of Nat. Hist. 1877, 4, vol. 19, p. 500.—Port Elizabeth, &c.

DEFRANCIA AMPLEXA, *Gould*, Proc. Boston Soc. Nat. Hist. vol. vii. 338.—Simon's Bay and Port Elizabeth.

DEFRANCIA CAPENSIS, *E. A. Smith*, pl. 4, fig. 84 ; Ann. and Mag. of Nat. Hist. 1882, vol. x. p. 296.—Port Elizabeth.

DEFRANCIA PONSONBYI, *Sowerby*, nov. sp. pl. 1, fig. 5. Testa breviuscula, valide clathrata, albida, spira turrita; anfractus 6 convexi, superne angulati, costis longitudinalibus elevatis rotundatis (in anfr. ult. 10), liris spiralibus angustioribus (in anfr. penult. 4) sculpti; anfractus ultimus leviter inflatus, infra medium contractus, vix productus, fascia fulva obscura pictus; apertura latiuscula; labrum leviter incrassatum, superne sinu brevissimo emargiuatum. Long. 6½, diam. maj. 3 millim.

Hab. Port Elizabeth.

This species somewhat resembles *D. linearis* (Mont.), but the lattice sculpture is much coarser.

MANGILIA CLATHRATA, *M. de Serres*, Journal de Conch. 1883, p. 327; Tryon's Manual of Conch. vol. vi. pl. 16, figs. 68–70.—This Mediterranean species has been found at Port Elizabeth.

MANGILIA COSTATA, *Donovan*, Sowb. Ill. Index of Brit. Shells, pl. 19, figs. 20, 21.—Specimens from Algoa Bay scarcely differ from those found on the English coasts.

MANGILIA COSTULATA, *Blainville*, var. *striolata* (Scacchi), Tryon, Man. of Conch. vol. v. pl. 21, fig. 19.—This well-known European shell has been found at Port Elizabeth.

MANGILIA SEPTANGULARIS, *Montagu*, Sowb. Ill. Index of Brit. Shells, pl. 19, fig. 24.—Mr. Crawford has found a specimen of this well-known British species in good condition at Port Elizabeth.

MITROMORPHA VOLVA, *Sowerby*, nov. sp. pl. 1, fig. 16. Testa elongato-fusiformis, alba; spira elatiuscula, ad apicem obtusa; anfractus 5½, levissime convexi, spiraliter dense lirati; anfractus ultimus spiram paulo superans, basin versus attenuatus; apertura oblonga; columella vix contorta; labrum rectiusculum, vix sinuatum. Long. 6, diam. maj. 2¼ millim.

Hab. Port Elizabeth.

Allied to the Japanese *M. lirata* (A. Adams), but shorter in proportion to its width, and more fusiform.

TRITON CUTACEUS, *Linn.* Reeve, Conch. Icon. (Triton), sp. 39—Port Elizabeth. The typical form of this common Mediterranean species is rare on the South African coast.

TRITON CUTACEUS, var. *Africana = Triton africanus* (A. Adams). See note, Journ. of Conch. vol. vi. p. 150.—Port Elizabeth.

TRITON CUTACEUS, var. *Doliarius* = *Triton doliarius* (Lamarck), Reeve, Conch. Icon. fig. 56. See note, Journ. of Conch. vol. vi. p. 150.—Port Elizabeth, &c. (common).

TRITON KLENEI, *Sowerby*, pl. 4, fig. 87; Journ. of Conch. vol. vi. p. 150.—Port Elizabeth.

TRITON NODIFER, . *Lamarck*, Reeve, Conch. Icon. sp. 9. Krauss (Sudafr. Mol. p. 114) quotes this shell as *F. Saulice* (Reeve, sp. 17).—I have very similar specimens from Japan, and cannot find any reliable character by which to distinguish them from the Mediterranean species.

TRITON AUSTRALIS (?), *Lamarck*, Reeve, Conch. Icon. sp. 12.—Krauss (Sudafr. Moll. p. 114) quotes this species from the Cape, but it may be that he has mistaken a form of *T. nodifer* for it.

TRITON LABIOSUS, *Wood*, Reeve, Conch. Icon. sp. 52 a.— Natal. A species of very wide distribution : Japan, Philippines, Australia, Mauritius, &c.

TRITON OLEARIUS, *Deshayes*, Reeve, Conch. Icon. sp. 32 = *T. succinctus* (Lamk.).—This species is quite common on the South African coast, and appears to be of almost world-wide distribution. I have had it from Japan, Australia, Red Sea, Mediterranean, West Indies, and Brazil.

TRITON EXARATUS, *Reeve*, Conch. Icon. fig. 50 a.—A rather young specimen from Port Elizabeth, not so angular as the Australian type. The shell somewhat resembles *T. cutaceus*, but has a longer rostrum.

TRITON RUBECULA, *Lamarck*, Reeve, Conch. Icon. fig. 29a. —Natal (Crawford). Common on the Mauritian coast.

TRITON PILEARIS, *Lamarck*, Reeve, Conch. Icon. sp. 23.— Natal coast (Krauss).

TRITON AQUATILIS, *Reeve*, Conch. Icon. sp. 24. Krauss quotes this as a variety of *T. pilearis*.

TRITON ÆGROTUS, *Reeve*, Proc. Zool. Soc. 1843; Conch. Icon. sp. 42.—Natal. This species is not uncommon on the Mauritian coast. Reeve quotes 'China' as the habitat.

TRITON PILETILIS, *Hinds*, Proc. Zool. Soc. 1844; Zool. Voy. Sulphur, Moll. p. 12, pl. 4, figs. 11, 12.—Agulhas Bank, 50 to 60 fath. (Hinds).

TRITON VESPACEUS, *Lamarck*, Reeve, Conch. Icon. sp. 61. —Natal coast (Krauss).

TRITON (EPIDROMUS) NITIDULUS, *Sowerby*, var. See Journ. of Conch. vol. vi. p. 7.—Port Elizabeth.

RANELLA LEUCOSTOMA, *Lamarck*, var. See Journal of Conch. vol. v. p. 10.—Port Elizabeth. The black markings on the lip of the South African variety are perfectly constant, and always distinguish it from the Australian form.

RANELLA ARGUS, *Lamarck*, Reeve, Conch. Icon. sp. 12.— Port Elizabeth. *R. vexillum* (Sowb.) is only a variety of this species. I have had several varieties from New Zealand, &c.

RANELLA GRANIFERA, *Lamarck*, Reeve, Conch. Icon. pl. 6. fig. 30. *Triton graniferum* (Q. et Gaim.).—Port Elizabeth (Crawford).

RANELLA GRANIFERA, *var.* = *R. livida* (Reeve), Conch. Icon. fig. 28.—Natal coast (Krauss).

RANELLA SEMIGRANOSA, *Lamarck*, Reeve, Conch. Icon. fig. 25.—Port Elizabeth (a living specimen). It may be doubted whether this is really a species distinct from R. granifera, but it is of a narrower form, and the granules are very small and partly obsolete. I have had it from the West Indies.

RANELLA LAMELLOSA, *Dunker*, Proc. Zool. Soc. 1862, p. 240 (as *Bursa l.*).—Port Elizabeth (a worn specimen), Japan (Dunker).

RANELLA CRUMENA, *Lamarck*, Reeve, Conch. Icon. sp. 17. —Natal. Common in the Indian Ocean. I have as yet only seen one specimen from South Africa.

RANELLA SIPHONATA, *Reeve*, Conch. Icon. sp. 28.—Natal coast (Krauss).

RANELLA PUSILLA, *Broderip*, Reeve, Conch. Icon. sp. 44, fig. 44a.—Natal coast (Wahlberg).

COMINELLA ANGLICANA, *Martini* (Buccinum), Reeve, Conch. Icon. sp. 23.—Table Bay. This is not an English species.

COMINELLA CAPENSIS, *Dunker*, Tryon, Manual of Conchology, vol. iii. pl. 73, fig. 260.— Port Elizabeth, &c.

C

COMINELLA (?) ANGUSTA. *Sowerby*, pl. I, fig. 8; Journ. of Conch. vol. v. p. 6.—Port Elizabeth.

COMINELLA LIMBOSA, *Reeve* (Buccinum), Conch. Icon. pl. 5, fig. 35.—Natal coast (Krauss), Table Bay, &c.

COMINELLA PAPYRACEA. *Bruguière = Buccinum intinctum* (Reeve), Conch. Icon. pl. 5, fig. 32.—Cape, and Natal coast (Krauss).

COMINELLA VIOLACEA, *Quoy et Gaim.* (Buccinum). Voy. de l'Astrol. Moll. pl. 30, figs. 32-34; Krauss, Sudafr. Moll. p. 120.—Table Bay (Quoy and Gaimard).

COMINELLA DELALANDII. *Kiener* (Buccinum), Coq. Viv. p. 15, pl. 5, fig. 14.—Cape (Kiener).

COMINELLA GLANDIFORMIS. *Reeve* (Buccinum), Conch. Icon. sp. 109.—South Africa ?.

COMINELLA SEMISULCATA, *Sowerby*, nov. sp. pl. I, fig. 7.— Testa subfusiformis, antice ventricosa, postice acuminata, fusca ; spira turrita, apice acutiusculo ; anfractus 7, leviter convexi, superne canaliculati, inferne spiraliter sulcati, aliter minute striati ; sutura lira angusta marginata : anfractus ultimus leviter inflatus, infra medium sulcis angustis circ. 10 sculptus ; apertura ovata, alba, columella arcuata, alba ; peristoma simplex, vix incrassatum. Long. 50 : diam. maj. 24 millim. ; apertura longa 22, lata 12.

Hab. Port Elizabeth.

This species, of which I have only seen one specimen (collected by Mr. Crawford), differs from its congeners, *C. porcata* and *C. lagenaria*, principally in the upper half of the whorls being smooth, and the lower half spirally grooved.

COMINELLA DUNKERI, *Küster*, Conch. Cab. (Buccinum), pl. 15, figs. 9-11.

COMINELLA LAGENARIA, *Deshayes* (Buccinum), Reeve, Conch. Icon. (Buccinum), pl. 5, figs. 33, 34.—Common at Port Elizabeth. Var. = *Purpura dubia* (Krauss), Sudafr. Moll., p. 117. – Port Elizabeth.

COMINELLA PORCATA, *Gmelin* (Buccinum), Reeve, Conch. Icon. pl. 4, fig. 22 = *Buccinum ligatum* (Kiener).—Port Elizabeth.

COMINELLA ELONGATA, *Dunker* (Buccinum), Proc. Zool. Soc. 1856, p. 356.—Port Elizabeth, Simon's Bay, &c.

COMINELLA TIGRINA, *Kiener* (Buccinum), Coq. Viv. p. 27, pl. 10.—Port Elizabeth, Table Bay, Simon's Bay, &c.

COMINELLA (?) PUNCTURATA, *Sowerby*, pl. 1, fig. 9; Journ. of Conch. vol. v. p. 4.—Port Elizabeth. I am uncertain as to the true generic position of this species.

COMINELLA (?) UNIFASCIATA, *Sowerby*, pl. 1, fig. 11; Journ. of Conch. vol. v. p. 5.—Port Elizabeth. The generic position of this species is doubtful.

COMINELLA (?) SULCATA, *Sowerby*, nov. sp. pl. 1, fig 10. —Testa elongata, angusta, pallide fulva, fusco obscure maculata; spira elongata, turrita; sutura impressa; anfractus 6, planato-convexi, ubique spiraliter profunde sulcati; anfractus ultimus vix inflatus; apertura oblonga, parviuscula; columella rectiuscula; peristoma simplex. Long. 10; diam. maj. 3 millim.; apert. long. 3½, lat. 1¼.

Var β. Testa minor, subpellucida, fusca.

Hab. Port Elizabeth.

This species belongs to the same group as *C. puncturata* and *C. angusta*, which I only place provisionally in the genus *Cominella*.

BULLIA LÆVIGATA, *Martini* (Buccinum), Reeve, Conch. Icon. (Bullia), sp. 6.—Port Elizabeth.

BULLIA RHODOSTOMA, *Gray*, Reeve, Conch. Icon. (Buccinum), sp. 25.—Port Elizabeth, &c.

BULLIA DIGITALIS, *Meusch.* (Buccinum), Reeve, Conch. Icon. (Bullia) sp. 4 = *Buccinum achatinum* (Lamarck). Varieties—*B. sulcata*, Reeve, Conch. Icon. sp. 14; *B. semiflammea*, Reeve, Conch. Icon. sp. 17; *B. semiusta*, Reeve, Conch. Icon. sp. 22.—Port Elizabeth.

BULLIA ANNULATA, *Lamarck*, Reeve, Conch. Icon. (Buccinum), sp. 13.—Port Elizabeth, &c. (common).

BULLIA CALLOSA, *Wood*, Reeve, Conch. Icon. sp. 24.—Port Elizabeth, &c.

BULLIA TENUIS, *Gray*, Reeve, Conch. Icon. sp. 1.—Port Elizabeth.

BULLIA PURA, *Melvill*, Journ. of Conch. vol. vi. p. 316.—Port Elizabeth.

BULLIA DILUTA, *Krauss*, Tryon, Man. of Conch. vol. iv. pl. 6, figs. 96, 97.—Port Elizabeth.

BULLIA NATALENSIS, *Krauss* (Buccinum), Sudafr. Moll. p. 121, pl. 6, fig. 16.—Natal coast (Krauss).

NASSA PULCHELLA, *A. Adams*, Proc. Zool. Soc. 1851; Reeve, Conch. Icon. sp. 90.—Port Elizabeth, Simon's Bay, and Cape coast generally.

NASSA SEROTINA, *A. Adams*, Proc. Zool. Soc. 1851, p. 108; Reeve, Conch. Icon. sp. 107.—Simon's Bay, Port Elizabeth, &c.

NASSA COCCINEA, *A. Adams*, MSS.?—Cape coast generally.

NASSA PLICOSA, *Dunker* (Buccinum), Krauss, Sudafr. Moll. p. 122, pl. 6. fig. 19. = *Nassa speciosa* (A. Adams).—Port Elizabeth.

NASSA BICALLOSA, *Smith*, Journ. Linn. Soc. xii. pl. 30, fig. 1.—Natal.

NASSA PLICATELLA, *A. Adams*, Proc. Zool. Soc. 1851, p. 111; Reeve, Conch. Icon. sp. 56.—Natal.

NASSA KRAUSSIANA, *Dunker* (Buccinum), Zeit. Mal. iii. 1846, p. 111.—Common at Port Elizabeth.

NASSA ARCULARIA, *Linn.*—A common well-known species, widely distributed in the Indian and Pacific Oceans, seldom found at Port Elizabeth, but, according to Krauss, very abundant in the Bay of Natal.

NASSA CAPENSIS, *Dunker* (Buccinum), Zeitschr. fur Malakozool. 1846, p. 110. ?= *N. pulchella*.—Cape of Good Hope (Dunker).

NASSA MARGINULATA, *Lamarck* (Buccinum), Reeve, Conch. Icon. sp. 43.—Natal Bay (Krauss). Common in the Indian Ocean.

NASSA CORONATA, *Bruguière*, Reeve, Conch. Icon. sp. 20. —Natal coast, rare (Krauss). Common in the Indian Ocean.

NASSA MYRISTICA, *Hinds*, Zool. Voy. Sulphur, Moll. p. 36, pl. 9, figs. 10, 11. --Cape (Hinds).

NASSA TRIFASCIATA, *A. Adams*, Proc. Zool. Soc. 1851, p. 113. (? = *N. labiosa*, J. Sowerby).—Several specimens in good condition from Port Elizabeth. The original type came from Vigo Bay. It is doubtful whether Marrat's *N. vincta* from West Africa is really distinct.

NASSA SULCIFERA, *A. Adams*, Reeve, Conch. Icon. sp. 24. —Algoa Bay (Reeve).

NASSA CRAWFORDI, *Sowerby*, nov. sp. pl. 4, fig. 86.—Testa elongato-acuminata, albida, lineis transversis fuscis pulcherrime ornata; spira acuminata, apice acuto; anfractus 6, convexi, sutura leviter impressa, vix crenulata sejuncti, eximie plicati; anfractus ultimus leviter inflatus, superne plicatus, plicis infra medium evanidis. Apertura ovata; fauce fusco lineata; peristoma simplex; columella contorta, duplicata. Long. 12; diam. maj. 5½ millim.
Hab. Port Elizabeth.
A lovely little shell, of which I have only seen a single specimen, found by Mr. Crawford. It may well be distinguished from its congeners by the delicate plication of the whorls, and the exquisite arrangement of brown lines with which it is ornamented.

DEMOULIA ABBREVIATA, *Wood* (Buccinum), Reeve, Conch. Icon., Nassa, sp. 194.—Port Elizabeth.

DEMOULIA RETUSA, *Lamarck* (Buccinum), Reeve, Conch. Icon., Nassa, sp. 195.—Port Elizabeth.

DEMOULIA PYRAMIDALIS, *A. Adams*, Proc. Zool. Soc. 1851; Reeve, Conch. Icon., Nassa, sp. 191.—Port Elizabeth.

EBURNA PAPILLARIS, *Sowerby*, Conch. Illust. Eburna, No. 1, fig. 1; Thes. Conch. vol. iii. pl. 215, fig. 7.—Port Elizabeth.

TEINOSTOMA LUCIDUM, *A. Adams*, Ann. and Mag. Nat. Hist. 1863, vol. xi. p. 267; Thes. Conch. vol. iii. pl. 256, figs. 49, 50.—Port Elizabeth.

PURPURA SQUAMOSA, *Lamarck*, Reeve, Conch. Icon. pl. 10, fig. 48.—Port Elizabeth and Natal coast.

PURPURA SUCCINCTA, *Lamarck*, Reeve, Conch. Icon. pl. 5, fig. 23.—Cape (Krauss). I have not met with this species from the Cape, but it is common in various localities, from Madagascar eastward.

PURPURA CINGULATA, *Linné* (Buccinum), Reeve, Conch. Icon. fig. 76.—Cape, Natal coast, and Port Elizabeth.   This curious species appears to be peculiar to the South African coast.

PURPURA CATARACTA, *Chemnitz* (Buccinum), Reeve, Conch. Icon., Purpura, sp. 40.—Port Elizabeth, Simon's Bay, &c.

PURPURA CAPENSIS, *Petit*, Journ. de Conch. 1852, pl. 7, fig. 6; Küster, Purpura, pl. 23a, fig. 6.   See Journ. of Conch. vol. v. p. 7.—Having seen an undoubted specimen of *Purpura luteostoma* collected at Port Elizabeth by Mr. Crawford, I am not sure that this is not a variety of the same, although, taking the typical forms, the differences are very great.

PURPURA LUTEOSTOMA, *Deshayes*, Lamarck, tom. x. p. 98; Reeve, Conch. Icon. sp. 35.—Port Elizabeth (Crawford).

PURPURA SCOBINA, *Quoy*, Zool. Voy. Astrolabe, pl. 38, figs. 19–21.—Port Elizabeth.   See Journ. of Conch. vol. vi. p. 148.

PURPURA TRIGONA, *Reeve*, Conch. Icon. Purpura, sp. 53. —Port Elizabeth.

PURPURA MANCINELLA, *Lamarck*, Reeve, Conch. Icon. pl. 2, fig. 7.—Natal coast (Krauss).   This species, common in the Indian Ocean and East Indian Archipelago, I have not met with from the Cape.

PURPURA BUFO, *Lamarck*, Reeve, Conch. Icon. pl. 2, fig. 7.—Natal coast (Krauss).   I have had this common species from China, Philippines, Travancore, and Madagascar, but not yet from South Africa.

PURPURA ZEYHERI, *Krauss*, Wiegmann's Archiv für Natur. 1852, p. 35.—Cape Coast (Krauss).   This species is unknown to me.

PURPURA PERSICA, *Lamarck*, Reeve, Conch. Icon. pl. 2, fig. 7.—Natal coast (Krauss).

PURPURA RUDOLPHI, *Lamarck*, Reeve, Conch. Icon. fig. 10. —Natal coast (Krauss).

PURPURA LAPILLUS, *Lamarck*.—This very common European species is quoted by Krauss as 'Cape,' but I have received no confirmation of its living there.

PURPURA (VEXILLA) VEXILLUM, *Lamarck*; *Buccinum vexillum*, Reeve, Conch. Icon. fig. 79.—Natal coast (Wahlberg). Port Elizabeth (Bairstow). Not uncommon on the Mauritian coast.

SISTRUM ARACHNOIDES, *Lamarck*, Reeve, Conch. Icon. sp. 5. —Natal coast (Krauss). Common in various localities, from the Red Sea to the East Indian Archipelago and Polynesia.

SISTRUM MORUS, *Blainville*, Reeve, Conch. Icon. pl. 2, fig. 10.—Natal coast (Wahlberg). Various East Indian localities.

SISTRUM ASPERUM, *Lamarck*, Reeve, Conch. Icon. sp. 13.— Natal coast (Krauss).

SISTRUM GRANULATUM, *Duclos* (Purpura). Ann. des Scienc. Nat. tom. xxvi. pl. 2, fig. 2. *Purpura tuberculata*, Blainville, Ann. du Mus. tom. i. p. 201, pl. 9. fig. 3. *Ricinula tuberculata*, Reeve, Conch. Icon. pl. 2, fig. 11.—Natal coast, Port Elizabeth, Red Sea, and Indian Ocean.

SISTRUM ANAXARES, *Duclos* (Purpura), Reeve, Conch. Icon. (Ricinula), sp. 61.—Natal coast (Krauss), Red Sea, and Indian Ocean.

SISTRUM HEPTAGONALE, *Reeve*, Conch. Icon. (Ricinula), sp. 17.—Natal coast (Krauss). The specimen I have seen from Natal is very pale in colour.

SISTRUM FISCELLUM, *Chemnitz* (Murex), Reeve, Conch. Icon. (Ricinula), sp. 28.—Natal coast (Krauss), Mauritius, and various Indian localities.

SISTRUM ELATUM, *Blainville* (Purpura), Reeve, Conch. Icon. (Ricinula), sp. 27 = *R. ochrostoma* (Blainv.).—Natal coast (Krauss).

SISTRUM LIVIDUM, *Reeve* (Buccinum), Conch. Icon. sp. 87. —South Africa?.

PSEUDOLIVA ANCILLA, *Hanley*, pl. 1, fig. 13. Proc. Zool. Soc. 1859, p. 429; Sowerby, Journ. of Conch. vol. vi. p. 149, pl. 3. fig. 2.—Port Elizabeth.

PSEUDOMUREX MEYENDORFFI, *Calcara*, Cenno. Moll. Sicil. pl. 4, fig. 22.—Port Elizabeth (Crawford), Madeira (Pactel Cat.), Mediterranean.

SEPARATISTA GRAYI, *A. Adams*, Proc. Zool. Soc. 1850, p. 45.— Port Elizabeth (rare).

LATIAXIS NODOSUS, *A. Adams*, Proc. Zool. Soc. 1853, p. 98 (as *Rapana (Latiaxis)n.*); Sowerby, Thes. Conch. vol. v. pl. 424, fig. 17.—Port Elizabeth (Crawford), Philippines (A. Adams), Port Jackson (Angas).

MELAPIUM LINEATUM. *Lamarck* (Pyrula), E. A. Smith, Ann. and Mag. of Nat. Hist. 1889, vol. iii. p. 269 = *Buccinum bulbus* (Wood).—Port Elizabeth.

OLIVA CÆRULEA, *Bolten*, Thes. Conch. vol. iv. pl. 331, figs. 48-50 = *O. episcopalis*, Lamk.—Rare at Port Elizabeth, but common on various coasts of the Indian and Indo-Pacific Oceans.

OLIVA BULBOSA. *Bolten*, Thes. Conch. vol. iv. pl. 340, fig. 189 = *O. inflata* (Lamarck).—Port Elizabeth (Bairstow), Very common in many Indian and Indo-Pacific localities.

OLIVA CAPENSIS. *Sowerby*. Thes. Conch. vol. iv. pl. 351, fig. 469.—Cape of Good Hope.

ANCILLA OBTUSA. *Swainson*, Sowerby, Thes. Conch. vol. iii. pl. 211, fig. 16.—Port Elizabeth.

ANCILLA OBESA. *Sowerby*. Thes. Conch. vol. iii. pl. 213, figs. 44, 45.—Port Elizabeth, &c.

ANCILLA CINNAMOMEA. *Lamarck*. Sowerby, Thes. Conch. vol. iii. pl. 212, figs. 33-35.—Port Elizabeth, &c.

ANCILLA AUSTRALIS, *Sowerby*, Thes. Conch. vol. iii. pl. 211, figs. 1 and 2.—Port Elizabeth (dead shells). This species is common on the New Zealand coasts.

ANCILLA MARMORATA, *Reeve*, Conch. Icon. Ancillaria, sp. 32.—Port Elizabeth.

ANCILLA FASCIATA. *Reeve*, Conch. Icon. Ancillaria, sp. 44. —Port Elizabeth.

ANCILLA DIMIDIATA. *Sowerby*, Thes. Conch. vol. iii.
pl. 213, figs. 55 and 56.

ANCILLA PURA, *Sowerby*, nov. sp., pl. 1, fig. 15.—Testa
anguste ovata, solidiuscula, alba ; spira exserta, subacuminata,
sutura parum callosa; aufractus 4, levissime convexi; ultimus
elongatus, aliquanto inflatus, infra medium baltea callosa
latiuscula munita, supra balteam sulca partim cœlatam
cincta; columella abbreviata, contorta, plicata; apertura
subampla.

Long. 21, diam. maj. 9 millim.; apert. long. 14, lat. 4.
Hab. Port Elizabeth.

A pure white shell, of simple character, much narrower
than *A. fulva* and allied species.

FASCIOLARIA HEYNEMANNI, *Dunker*, Sowerby, Thes. Conch.
vol. v. pl. 425, fig. 11.= *F. purpurea* (Jonas). —Port Elizabeth. Rarely found in good condition.

FASCIOLARIA LUGUBRIS, *Reeve*, Conch. Icon. sp. 2. = *F.
badia*, Krauss, Sudafr. Moll. p. 110, pl. 6, fig. 12.—Natal
coast (Krauss).

LATIRUS BAIRSTOWI, *Sowerby*, pl. 1, fig. 18 ; Journal of
Conch. vol. v. p. 8.—Port Elizabeth.

LATIRUS ROUSI, *Sowerby*, pl. 1, fig. 19; Journal of Conch.
vol. v. p. 10.—Port Elizabeth.

LATIRUS (PERISTERNIA) INCARNATUS, *Reeve*, Conch. Icon.
Turbinella sp. 55. —Natal (Crawford).

LATIRUS (PERISTERNIA) LEUCOTHEA, *Melvill*, Mem. and
Proc. Manchester Lit. and Phil. Soc. vol. iv. series 4, p. 35,
pl. 2, fig. 15.—Natal (Crawford).

LATIRUS (PERISTERNIA) NASSATULUS, *Lamarck*, Reeve,
Conch. Icon. (Turbinella), sp. 45.—Natal coast (Krauss).
Widely distributed in the East Indies.

TURBINELLA TRUNCATA, *Sowerby*, nov. sp., pl. 4, fig. 85.
—Testa subcylindraceo-turbinata, solida, postice inflata,
obtuse angulata, truncata, antice leviter attenuata; alba,
epidermide scabrosa fusca induta, liris paucis irregularibus
spiraliter cincta, mediocriter umbilicata, apice obtuso,
mamillato, paulo elevato: spira fere plana; anfractus 8,
sublævigati, sutura anguste canaliculata discreti; apertura

D

elongata, angustiuscula, margine dextro paulo incrassato, hic
illic sparsim fusco maculato ; columella plicis 4, parviusculis
subæqualibus, leviter obliquis munita.

Long. 65, lat. maj. 50 millim. ; apertura longa 60, in
medio lata 13.

Hab. Port Elizabeth.

This is quite a new form of *Turbinella* in which the anterior portion answering to the rostrum in the typical form
(*T. pyrum*) is quite half as broad as the widest part of the
shell, and the anterior part of the aperture is so little narrower than the posterior, that it can scarcely be called a
canal. The four small, slightly oblique plaits are situated
about (or a little below) the middle of the columella.

The type specimen, which is in very good preservation,
is in the collection recently presented to the Oxford University Museum by S. D. Bairstow, Esq. I have long had a
specimen of the species, but in such bad condition that I
would not venture to describe it.

VOLUTA (CALLIPARA) BULLATA, *Swainson*, Thes. Conch.
vol. i. pl. 53, fig. 88.—Broken specimens not uncommon at
Port Elizabeth.

VOLUTA (VOLUTILITHES) ABYSSICOLA, *Adams & Reeve*,
Voy. of Samarang, Moll. p. 25, pl. 7, fig. 6.—Several full-sized
specimens of this remarkable form were taken in the voyage
of the 'Challenger,' which, with the young shell of the
'Samarang,' are all at present known.

VOLUTA AFRICANA, *Reeve*, P. Z. S. 1856, pl. 33, figs. 3, 4.
—Port Elizabeth (Bairstow). This rare species has not yet
been found in perfect condition.

MITRA PICTA, *Reeve*, Conch. Icon. species 123.—Port
Elizabeth. Dead shells pretty common.

MITRA SIMPLEX, *Dunker*, Zeitschr. für Malak. 1846,
p. 111 ; Krauss, Sudafr. Moll. p. 121, tab. 6, fig. 20. ? = *M.
patula*, Reeve, Conch. Icon. sp. 333.—Port Elizabeth.

MITRA CRATITIA, *A. Adams*, Proc. Zool. Soc. 1851, p. 132 ;
Thes. Conch. vol. iv. pl. 24, fig. 545.—Specimens in the
British Museum, said to be from South Africa.

MITRA LATRUNCULARIA, *Reeve*, Conch. Icon. sp. 166.—
Worn specimens not uncommon at Port Elizabeth.

MITRA CAPENSIS, *Dunker*, Reeve, Conch. Icon. pl. 23, fig. 268.—Port Elizabeth, &c.

MITRA MERULA, *Sowerby*, pl. 1. fig. 17 ; Journal of Conch. vol. vi. p. 8, pl. 1, fig. 11.—Port Elizabeth.

MITRA SCHRŒTERI, *Deshayes*, Sowerby, Thes. Conch. vol. iv. pl. 375, fig. 529.—S. Africa ?

MITRA ÆRUMNOSA, *Melvill*, Journal of Conch. 1888, vol. v p. 282, pl. 2, fig. 12.—Algoa Bay.

MITRA LIMBIFERA, *Lamarck*, Reeve, Conch. Icon. pl. 23, fig. 180a.—Natal coast (Krauss).

MITRA (IMBRICARIA) CARBONACEA, *Hinds*, Voy. Sulphur, Moll. p. 41, pl. 11, figs. 9. 10 ; Sowerby, Thes. Conch. vol. iv. pl. 369, fig. 356.—Agulhas Bank (Hinds).

MARGINELLA MOSAICA, *Sowerby*, Thes. Conch. vol. i. pl. 75, fig. 59.—Port Elizabeth.

—— Var. *Langleyi*, Sowerby.—A curious variety, in which the markings are merged into longitudinal streaks, waved so as to form a band in the middle of the body whorl.

MARGINELLA ORNATA, *Redfield*, American Journal of Conch. vol. vi. p. 246.= *M. vittata*, Reeve (non Edwards), Conch. Icon. sp. 17.= *M. serpentina* (Jousseaume).—Port Elizabeth. This species has been mistaken for *M. Poucheti* (Petit), and placed in various collections under that name. It is however totally different. *Vide* Journal de Conch. 1851, vol. ii. p. 46, pl. 1, fig. 3.

MARGINELLA PIPERATA, *Hinds*, Proc. Zool. Soc. 1844. p. 72 ; Sowerby, Thes. Conch. vol. i. pl. 75, figs. 40, 44.— Port Elizabeth.

—— Vars. *albocincta*, *strigata*, *lutea* and *lineata*, Sowerby, J. of C. vol. vi. p. 8. —Port Elizabeth.

MARGINELLA BAIRSTOWI, *Sowerby*. pl. 1, fig. 23 ; J. of C. vol. v. p. 11, 1886, vol. vi. pl. 1, fig. 3.—Port Elizabeth.

MARGINELLA LINEOLATA, *Sowerby*, pl. 1. fig. 24 ; J. of C. vol. v. p. 11, 1886, vol. vi. pl. 1, fig. 2.—Port Elizabeth.

MARGINELLA FLOCCATA, *Sowerby*, pl. 1, fig. 25 ; J. of C. vol. vi. p. 8, 1889, pl. 1, fig. 4.—Port Elizabeth.

MARGINELLA PAXILLUS, *Reeve*, Conch. Icon. sp. 133.—Port Elizabeth.

MARGINELLA PELLICULA, *Marrat*, Weinkauff, in Küster, Conch. Cab. Marg. pl. 23, figs. 11, 12.—Port Elizabeth.

MARGINELLA ZONATA, *Kiener*, p. 41, pl. 13, fig. 4 ; var. *bilineata*, Krauss, Sudafr. Moll. p. 126, tab. 6, fig. 22.—Port Elizabeth.

MARGINELLA DUNKERI, *Krauss*, Sudafr. Moll. p. 126, tab. 6, fig. 23.—Port Elizabeth.

MARGINELLA CAPENSIS, *Dunker*. Krauss, Sudafr. Moll. p. 125, tab. 6, fig. 21.—Cape coast (Krauss).

MARGINELLA METCALFEI, *Angas*, Proc. Zool. Soc. 1877, p. 173, pl. 26, fig. 8.—Port Jackson (Angas), Port Elizabeth.

MARGINELLA INCONSPICUA, *Sowerby*, Thes. Conch. vol. i. pl. 75, fig. 80.—Port Elizabeth.

MARGINELLA SAVIGNYI, *Issel*, Moll. Mar. Rosso, p. 115, 1869 ; Savig. Descript. de l'Egypte, Coq. pl. 6, fig. 18.—Port Elizabeth.

MARGINELLA NEGLECTA, *Sowerby*, Thes. Conch. vol. i. pl. 75, fig. 135.—Port Elizabeth, Mauritius, &c.

MARGINELLA CYLINDRICA, *Sowerby*, Thes. Conch. vol. i. pl. 76, fig. 134.—Port Elizabeth.

MARGINELLA PYRUM, *Gronovius*, Reeve, Conch. Icon. sp. 13. = *N. nubecula*, Sowerby, Thes. Conch. vol. i. pl. 75, fig. 51.—A large dead shell in Bairstow's collection. Port Elizabeth ?.

MARGINELLA CHRYSEA, *Watson*, Gastrop. of Challenger, p. 267, pl. 16, fig. 8. - Cape Town and Port Elizabeth.

. MARGINELLA EPIGRUS, *Reeve*, Conch. Icon. sp. 151.—Cape of Good Hope.

MARGINELLA BULBOSA, *Reeve*. Conch. Icon. sp. 144.—Cape of Good Hope.

MARGINELLA KEENI, *Marrat*, Ann. and Mag. of Nat. Hist. 1871, vol. vii. p. 141, pl. 11, fig. 13.

MARGINELLA ROSEA, *Lamarck*, Sowerby, Thes. Conch. vol. i. pl. 55, fig. 56.—Cape and Natal coast (Krauss).

MARGINELLA BIPLICATA, *Krauss*, Archiv für Nat. 1852, p. 37.—A small semipellucid species with which I am unacquainted. Cape Coast (Krauss).

MARGINELLA MULTIZONA, *Krauss*, Archiv für Nat. 1852, p. 37.—A small species with 10 to 15 red zones. I have not met with this shell. Cape Coast (Krauss).

MARGINELLA REEVEI, *Krauss*, Archiv für Nat. 1852, p. 38. —A minute fusiform species, conical spire, pale red zones, 4-plaited columella. Cape Coast (Krauss). Unknown to me.

MARGINELLA ZEYHERI, *Krauss*, Archiv für Nat. 1852, p. 38.—A small ovate solid white species, with a short conical spire, wide mouth, and columella with four equal plaits. Unknown to me. Cape Coast (Krauss).

MARGINELLA CRASSILABRUM, *Sowerby*, Thes. Conch. vol. i. pl. 76, figs. 124, 125.—Port Elizabeth.

MARGINELLA ELECTRINA, *Sowerby*, n. sp., pl. 1, fig. 22.— Testa cylindraceo-fusiformis, tenuis, pellucida, fulva; spira breviter conica, obtusa; anfractus 4, leviter convexi; sutura callosa; anfractus ultimus elongatus, leviter convexus, basin versus leviter attenuatus; apertura angusta, antice latior; labrum inflexum leviter incrassatum, paulo marginatum, rectiusculum; columella basi contorta, triplicata,

Long. 12, diam. maj. 7 millim.; sp. min. longa 8, diam. 4½ millim.

Hab. Port Elizabeth.

ERATO SULCIFERA, *Gray*, Sowerby, Conch. Illust. Cypræa, p. 15, fig. 46.—Cape (Gray).

COLUMBELLA ALBUGINOSA, *Reeve*, Conch. Icon. sp. 223. - Port Elizabeth.

COLUMBELLA CEREALIS, *Menke* (Buccinum), Krauss, Sudafr. Moll. p. 122, tab. 6, fig. 17. = *C. Kraussii*, Sowerby, Thes. Conch. vol. i. pl. 40, fig. 180.—Port Elizabeth and Simon's Bay.

COLUMBELLA SAGENA, *Reeve*, Conch. Icon. sp. 162.—Port Elizabeth. A Japanese species.

COLUMBELLA PULCHELLA, *Sowerby*, Thes. Conch. vol. i. pl. 39, figs. 121, 122.—Port Elizabeth. Known as a West Indian species.

COLUMBELLA FLAVA, *Bruguière*, Reeve,Conch. Icon. sp. 27, fig. 27a. Variety *C. undata*, Duclos, Kiener Col. p. 27, pl. 9, fig. 1.—Common in the Indian Ocean, rare at Port Elizabeth.

COLUMBELLA FLOCCATA, *Reeve*, Conch. Icon. sp. 160.— Port Elizabeth, Buffalo, Cape Colony (Reeve).

COLUMBELLA VARIANS, *Sowerby*, Thes. Conch. vol. i. pl. 37, fig. 47.—Port Elizabeth.

COLUMBELLA BIFLAMMATA, *Reeve*, Conch. Icon. sp. 226.— Port Elizabeth.

COLUMBELLA TURTURINA, *Lamarck*, Sowerby, Thes. Conch. vol. i. pl. 37, figs. 38-40.—Natal coast (Krauss). Common in various places, from Mauritius to the Philippine Islands.

COLUMBELLA LACTEA, *Duclos*, Reeve, Conch. Icou. sp. 120. —Natal coast (Krauss).

COLUMBELLA MENDICARIA, *Lamarck*, var.? Kiener, Coq. Viv. pl. 6, fig. 1a.—Natal coast (Krauss).

COLUMBELLA CAPENSIS, *Sowerby*, n. sp., pl. 1, fig. 20.— Testa fusiformis, tenuis, alba; spira acuta, apice papillari; anfractus 5½ convexiusculi, longitudinaliter multiplicati, striis angustis et confertis spiraliter sculpti; anfractus ultimus inflatus, basin versus attenuatus; columella leviter contorta, haud callosa; apertura lata, labrum arcuatum, tenue.

Long. 10, diam. maj. 5 millim.

Hab. Port Elizabeth.

A white species of the 'Anachis' section, allied to *C. pulchella*.

COLUMBELLA ALGOENSIS, *Sowerby*, n. sp., pl. 1, fig. 21.— Testa elongata, turrita, fulva, lineis fuscis transversis interruptis hic illic textiliformibus picta, antice fusco-zonata; spira percelata, apice papillari; sutura impressa; anfractus 5, convexiusculi, longitudinaliter irregulariter plicati; spiraliter dense sulcati; anfractus ultimus angustus; columella leviter recurva; apertura parva, labrum tenue. Long. 8, diam. maj. 2¾ millim. This shell has somewhat the appearance of a

Defrancia, but upon examination I have come to the conclusion that it belongs to the same section as the foregoing.

ALCIRA ELEGANS, *H. Adams*, Proc. Zool. Soc. 1860, p. 451 ; Tryon, M. of C. vol. v. p. 188, pl. 61, fig. 9.

HARPA MINOR, *Lamarck*, var. *crassa*, Philippi.—Cape coast (Phil.). The several varieties of this species are pretty widely distributed in the Indian and Pacific Oceans, but I have not yet met with it from the Cape.

CASSIS TESTICULUS, *Linné*, Reeve, Conch. Icon. sp. 10. —A specimen of this well-known West Indian and West African species in Bairstow collection from South Africa.

CASSIS ACHATINA, *Lamarck*, Reeve, Conch. Icon. sp. 28. —Several varieties of this species are found at Port Elizabeth, and probably the shell quoted by Krauss as *C. Zeylanica* (Lamk.) is one of these.

DOLIUM LUTEOSTOMA, *Küster*, Conch. Cab. pl. 58, fig. 1. —This species was quoted by me in the 'Journal of Conchology,' as *D. Favanni* (Hanley), from which I find it differs. It is nearly allied to *D. variegatum*. The South-African specimens differ very little from the Japanese.

LAMELLARIA PERSPICUA, *Linn.*, Sowerby's Illust. Index of Brit. Shells, pl. 16, figs. 23, 24.—Port Elizabeth.

NATICA IMPERFORATA, *Sowerby* (Gray ?), Zool. of Captain Beechey's Voyage, p. 135, pl. 37, fig. 1 ; Sowerby, Thes. Conch. vol. v. pl. 460, fig. 93. = *N. genuana*, Reeve, Conch. Icon. sp. 121.—Common at Port Elizabeth.

NATICA FORATA, *Récluz*, Sowerby, Thes. Conch. vol. v. pl. 460, fig. 96.—Port Elizabeth, Buffalo River, &c.

NATICA DIDYMA, *Bolten*, Sowerby, Thes. Conch. vol. v. pl. 455, fig. 14. = N. Lamarckiana (Récluz).—Port Elizabeth (rare), Japan, Philippines, &c. (common).

NATICA SIMIÆ, *Chemnitz*, Sowerby, Thes. Conch. vol. v. pl. 459, fig. 71. -Port Elizabeth (rare).

NATICA MAMILLA, *Lamarck*, Chemnitz, Conch. Cab. Bd. v. tab. 189, figs. 1928, 1929 ; Sowerby, Thes. Conch. vol. v. pl. 456, fig. 29. Natal (Crawford). A common species, widely distributed in the Indian and Pacific Oceans.

NATICA PYGMÆA, *Philippi*, Abbild. und Beschreib. vol. i. p. 17, pl. 1, fig. 12.—Unknown to me. Table Bay (Krauss).

NATICA MAROCHIENSIS, *Gmelin*, Sowerby, Thes. Couch. vol. v. pl. 462, fig. 151.=*N. maroccana* (Chemnitz)=*N. lurida* (Philippi).—Natal (Crawford).

SCALARIA LACTEA, *Krauss*, Sudafr. Moll. p. 94, pl. 5, fig. 27 ; Conch. Icon. sp. 93.—Natal coast (Krauss); Port Elizabeth (Bairstow).

SCALARIA CLATHRATULA, *Montagu*, Sowerby, Illust. Index of Brit. Shells, pl. 15, fig. 20.—Several specimens of this British and European species found at Port Elizabeth.

SCALARIA FRAGILIS, *Hanley*, Sowerby, Thes. Conch. vol. i. pl. 33, fig. 64.—Port Elizabeth (a small specimen).

SCALARIA CORONATA, *Lamarck*, Sowerby, Thes. Conch. vol. i. pl. 35, fig. 133. -This species, generally known as West Indian, is not uncommon at Port Elizabeth.

SCALARIA PSEUDO-SCALARIS, *Brocchi*, = *S. clathrus*, Sowerby, Thes. Conch. vol. v. pl. 35, fig. 131.—A species of almost universal distribution : Britain, Mediterranean, Mauritius, East and West Indies, as well as South Africa.

SCALARIA FUCATA, *Pease*, Proc. Zool. Soc. 1860, p. 400.—Sandwich Islands (Pease).—Port Elizabeth.

SCALARIA REPLICATA, *Sowerby*, Thes. Conch. vol. i. pl. 32, figs. 23, 24. -Port Elizabeth (rare).

TEREBRA CAPENSIS, *E. A. Smith*, pl. 4, fig. 88 ; Ann. and Mag. Nat. Hist. 1873, vol. xi. p. 269.—Port Elizabeth.

TEREBRA GRAYI, *E. A. Smith*, pl. 4, fig. 89 ; Ann. and Mag. Nat. Hist. 1877, vol. xix. p. 227. = *T. gracilis* (Gray), name preoccupied.—South-east Africa.

TEREBRA PERTUSA, *Born*, Sowerby, Thes. Conch. vol. i. pl. 42, figs. 42, 43.—Port Elizabeth (rare).

TEREBRA TIARELLA, *Deshayes*, Reeve, Conch. Icon. sp. 109.—Natal.

TEREBRA CINGULIFERA, *Lamarck*, Sowerby, Thes. Conch. vol. i. pl. 42, fig. 24.—Port Elizabeth (rare), Mauritius, &c. (common).

OBELISCUS SULCATUS, *A. Adams*, Sowerby, Thes. Conch. vol. ii. pl. 171, fig. 31.—Port Elizabeth (rare). Common in the Indian Ocean.

SYRNOLA ACICULATA. *A. Adams* (Obeliscus), Sowerby, Thes. Conch. vol. ii. pl. 171, fig. 21.—Port Elizabeth (rare).

SYRNOLA CAPENSIS. *Sowerby.* nov. sp., pl. 2, fig. 35.— Testa subulata, luteo-fusca, polita, nitida; anfractus 12, levissime convexi, sutura impressa sejuncti; apertura ovalis; peristoma simplex; columella uniplicata.

Long. 12½, diam. maj. 3 millim.; apertura longa 2½, lata 1½ millim.

Hab. Port Elizabeth (Crawford).

RINGICULA AUSTRALIS, *Crosse*, Journ. de Conch. vol. xiii. p. 44, pl. 2, fig. 5.—S. Australia (Crosse). Port Elizabeth.

TURBONILLA ARGENTEA, *Sowerby*, n. sp., pl. 2, fig. 37.— Testa elongato-turrita, tenuis, argentea, nitens, longitudinaliter costata; costis numerosis, confertiusculis, leviter obliquis, interstitiis lævibus; spira acuta; anfractus 9—10, convexiusculi, sutura impressa sejuncti; anfractus ultimus parvus, costis circ. 20 instructus, ad basim rotundatus, lævigatus; apertura ovata; peristoma acutum; columella rectiuscula.

Long. 4½, diam. maj. 1 millim.

Hab. Port Elizabeth.

A little, shining, silvery white shell, shorter than *T. lactea* (Linn.) and more acutely turreted than *T. delicata* (Monterosato).

TURBONILLA LÆVICOSTATA, *Sowerby*, n. sp., pl. 2, fig. 36.— Testa elongato-turrita, lactea, longitudinaliter levissime costata, costis basin versus evanidis; spira acuta; anfractus 10, levissime convexi, sutura leviter impressa sejuncti; apertura ovata; peristoma acutum; columella leviter arcuata.

Long. 5½, diam. maj. 1½ millim.

Hab. Port Elizabeth.

Rather larger than the last species, with whorls less convex, and ribs almost obsolete.

TURBONILLA TEGULATA, *Sowerby*, n. sp., pl. 2, fig. 38. – Testa elongato-turrita, tenuiuscula, alba, subpellucida, undique conspicue decussata; spira acuta, turrita; anfractus 10, convexi, superne angulati, tabulati, spiraliter et longi-

E

tudinaliter sulcati, leviter granulati ; apertura rotunde ovata; columella leviter contorta ; peristoma acutum.

Long. 4½, diam. maj. 1¼ millim.

Hab. Port Elizabeth.

A turreted, shining white, decussated shell, with whorls slightly tabulated. The surface between the decussating grooves has a granulated appearance.

TURBONILLA CANDIDA, *A. Adams*, P.Z.S. 1853, p. 181.—Port Elizabeth.

TURBONILLA SCALARIS, *Philippi*, Sowb. Illust. Index of Brit. Shells, pl. 16, fig. 9 (as *Chemnitzia l.*).—Port Elizabeth.

TURBONILLA LACTEA, *Linn.*, Sowb. Illust. Index of Brit. Shells, pl. 16, fig. 1 (as *Chemnitzia l.*) = *Turbo elegantissimus.*—Port Elizabeth.

TURBONILLA CASTANEA, *Carpenter*, MSS.?—Port Elizabeth.

TURBONILLA RUFA, *Philippi*, Sowb. Ill. Index. Brit. Shells, pl. 16, figs. 4, 5. —Port Elizabeth.

TURBONILLA BIFASCIATA, *A. Adams*, Ann. and Mag. of Nat. Hist. vol. vii. p. 297 ; Tryon, Man. of Conch. vol. viii. pl. 76, fig. 47.—Port Elizabeth.

TURBONILLA FUSCA, *A. Adams*, P. Z. S. 1853, p. 181 ; Tryon, vol. viii. pl. 76, fig. 46.—Port Elizabeth. Tyron quotes *T. bifasciata* as a variety of this, but I think the author was right in considering the species distinct.

ODOSTOMIA ANGASI, *Tryon*, Man. of Conch. vol. viii. p. 362, pl. 79, fig. 68. = *O. lactea* (Angas), preoccupied by Dunker.—Port Jackson (Angas). Port Elizabeth.

EULIMA SOLIDA, *Sowerby*, Conch. Icon. sp. 18.—Port Elizabeth.

EULIMA ATLANTICA, *E. A. Smith*, P. Z. S. 1890, p. 278, pl. 23, fig. 25.—St. Helena and Port Elizabeth.

EULIMA NITIDA, *Lamarck*, Sowerby, Thes. Conch. vol. ii. pl. 169, fig. 17.—In the byssus of *Pinna squamifera* ; mouth of the Knysna River (Krauss).

EULIMA DISTORTA, *Deshayes*, Sowb. Thes. Conch. vol. ii. pl. 169, fig. 6.—Port Elizabeth.

EULIMA LANGLEYI, *Sowerby*, n. sp., pl. 1, fig. 31. —Testa elongata, angusta, recta, pellucida, polita; spira acuta; anfractus 8–9, levissime convexi; sutura contecta; area suturalis fascia pellucida notata ; anfractus ultimus oblongus, vix inflatus; apertura oblongo-ovata ; peristoma simplex.
Long. 4¼, diam. maj. 1¼ millim.
Hab. Port Elizabeth.
A minute, straight species, in form resembling *E. intermedia*, Jeffreys.

CINGULINA CIRCINATA, *A. Adams*, Ann. and Mag. of Nat. Hist. 1860, vol. vi. p. 414.—Port Elizabeth. The specimens are scarcely distinguishable from the Japanese.

CINGULINA ACUTILIRATA, *Sowerby*, nov. sp., pl. 1, fig. 32.— Testa elongata, turrita, alba ; spira recta, levissime convexa, versus apicem acuta ; anfractus 9–10 vix convexi, liris 3–4, acutis spiraliter cingulati; apertura parviuscula, subovata ; columella rectiuscula ; labrum acutum.
Long. 5, diam. maj. 1½ millim.
Hab. Port Elizabeth.
Differing from *C. circinata*, A. Adams, in the sharpness of the ridges and the absence of interstitial crenulation.

CERITHIOPSIS PURPUREA, *Angas*, P.Z.S. 1877, p. 36, pl. 5, fig. 7.—Port Elizabeth.

CERITHIOPSIS TUBERCULARIS, *Montagu*, Sowb. Illus. Index Brit. Shells, pl. 15, fig. 11.—Port Elizabeth.

DIALA CAPENSIS, *Sowerby*, pl. 1, fig. 28 ; Journ. of Conch. vol. vi. p. 12, pl. 1, fig. 17.—Port Elizabeth.

DIALA INFRASULCATA, *Sowerby*, nov. sp., pl. 1, fig. 30.— Testa pyramidata, fusca, aut sordide albida ; spira acuminata, acuta ; anfractus 8–9, planati, sutura impressa sejuncti ; anfractus ultimus angulatus, infra angulum convexus, spiraliter 6–7 sulcatus, angustissime umbilicatus ; apertura latiuscula ; peristoma simplex.
Long. 7, diam. maj. 2 millim.
Hab. Port Elizabeth.

DIALA DUBIA, *Sowerby*, nov. sp., pl. 1, fig. 29.—Testa oblonga, albida, lævigata ; spira acutiuscula, elata ; anfractus

6, leviter convexi, sutura impressa sejuncti; anfr. ult. rotundatus; apertura subcircularis; peristoma simplex.

Long. 4, diam. maj. 1¾ millim.

Hab. Port Elizabeth.

A simple little shell, of which the generic position is somewhat doubtful.

ACLIS TENUISTRIATA, *Sowerby*, nov. sp., pl. 2, fig. 56.— Testa elongata, angusta, alba; spira versus apicem acutissima; anfractus 8, levissime convexi, spiraliter multistriati, striis tenuissimis, confertis; sutura leviter impressa; anfractus ultimus oblongus; apertura leviter expansa; labrum tenue.

Long. 9, diam. maj. 2 millim.

Hab. Port Elizabeth.

A delicate little white shell, very finely striated, with an oval mouth and a perfectly plain columella.

SOLARIUM CINGULUM, *Kiener*, Sowerby, Thes. Conch. vol. iii. pl. 253, fig. 55.—Port Elizabeth.

SOLARIUM VARIEGATUM, *Gmelin* = *S. perspectiviunculus* (Chemnitz), Sowerby, Thes. Conch. vol. iii. pl. 254. fig. 60.— Natal (Crawford). Widely distributed in the Indian Ocean and South Pacific.

SOLARIUM CANCELLATUM, *Krauss*, Sudafr. Moll. p. 95, pl. 5, fig. 29.—Algoa Bay (Krauss).

IANTHINA GLOBOSA, *Swainson*, Sowerby, Thes. Conch. vol. v. pl. 444, figs. 16, 17.—St. Helena (Lesson), Port Elizabeth.

IANTHINA FRAGILIS, *Lamarck*, Sowb. Thes. Conch. vol. v. pl. 443, figs. 1-4.—Atlantic, Pacific, and Port Elizabeth.

IANTHINA EXIGUA, *Lamarck*, Sowb. Thes. Conch. vol. v. pl. 444, figs. 23, 24.—Atlantic, Mediterranean, and Algoa Bay.

IANTHINA UMBILICATA, *D'Orbigny*, Sowb. Thes. Conch. vol. v. pl. 444, sp. 22.—Algoa Bay.

RECLUZIA MONTROUZIERI, *Souverbie*, Journal de Conchyliologie, 1872, pl. 1, fig. 8.—New Caledonia (Mont), Port Elizabeth.

CONUS TINIANUS, *Hwass*, Sowerby, Thes. Conch. vol. iii. pl. 205, fig. 450; var. *C. aurora* (Lamarck), fig. 456; var.

C. rosaceus (Chemnitz), fig. 455; var. *C. Loveni* (Krauss), fig. 449.—Port Elizabeth.

CONUS INFRENATUS, *Reeve.* Conch. Icon. sp. 285; Sowb. Conch. Icon. vol. iii. pl. 205, figs. 451–453; var. *C. succinctus* (A. Adams). Thes. Conch. vol. iii. pl. 198, fig. 257. Port Elizabeth, &c.

CONUS PICTUS, *Reeve*, Conch. Icon. sp. 98. In Thes. Conch. fig. 444 represents *C. jaspideus.*—Port Elizabeth. Rarely seen in good condition.

CONUS GILVUS, *Reeve*, Conch. Icon. sp. 253. - Saldanha Bay, South Africa (Reeve).

CONUS CROTCHI, *Reeve*, Conch. Icon. sp. 254.— Saldanha Bay (Reeve).

CONUS LAUTUS, *Reeve*, Conch. Icon. sp. 255. Port Elizabeth. Only dead and somewhat worn specimens at present found.

CONUS ELONGATUS, *Chemnitz*, Sowb. Thes. Conch. vol. iii. pl. 204, figs. 140, 141. = *C. mozambicus* (Brug.).—Port Elizabeth (rare).

CONUS CAFFER, *Krauss*, Sudafr. Moll. p. 131, pl. 6, fig. 24; Sowb. Thes. Conch. vol. iii. pl. 205, figs. 246, 247. —I am not quite satisfied that this is distinct from *C. elongatus.* It is certainly not *C. pictus*, as suggested by Tryon.

CONUS ALGOENSIS, *Sowerby*, Thes. Conch. vol. iii. pl. 204, fig. 421.—Algoa Bay ?.

CONUS NATALENSIS, *Sowerby* (*natalis*), Thes. Conch. vol. iii. pl. 199, figs. 292, 293.—Natal (rare).

CONUS FULVUS, *Sowerby*, pl. 2, fig. 34; Journ. of Conch. vol. vi. p. 10, pl. 1, fig. 1.—Port Elizabeth. I have only seen one specimen of this species, which is in the collection of Mr. Bairstow.

CONUS BAIRSTOWI, *Sowerby*, pl. 2, fig. 33; Journ. of Conch. vol. vi. p. 9, pl. 1, fig. 12.—Port Elizabeth (Mus. Bairstow).

CONUS HEBRÆUS, *Linn.*, Sowerby, Thes. Conch. vol. iii. pl. 189, fig. 56.—Natal coast (Krauss). Common in the Indian Ocean.

CONUS BETULINUS, *Linn.*, Sowb. Thes. Conch. vol. iii. pl. 197, fig. 244.—Natal (Crawford). Common in the Indian Ocean.

CONUS TESSELLATUS, *Born*, Sowb. Thes. Conch. vol. iii. pl. 198, fig. 250.—Natal (Crawford).

CONUS NEMOCANUS, *Hwass.* · A specimen in the Bairstow Collection from South Africa.

CONUS LIVIDUS, *Linn.*, Sowerby, Thes. Conch. vol. iii. pl. 188, fig. 27.—Natal coast (Krauss). One of the commonest shells on various coasts from the Red Sea and Mauritius to the Philippine and South Sea Islands. I have not yet met with it from South Africa.

CONUS MINIMUS, *Linn.*, Sowerby, Thes. Conch. vol. iii. pl. 189, fig. 154.—Natal coast (Krauss). This species is also widely distributed on the Indian and Indo-Pacific coasts, but I have not seen it among South African shells.

CONUS TEXTILE, *Linn.*, Thes. Conch. vol. iii. pl. 209, fig. 567.—Natal (Bairstow). A typical specimen in the collection at Oxford.

CONUS CONSPERSUS, *Reeve*, Conch. Icon. sp. 262, var. *C. Verreauxi* (Kiener), Krauss, Wiegmann's Archiv für Naturgeschichte, 1852, p. 39.—Cape (Krauss).

CONUS ALTISPIRATUS, *Sowerby*, Proc. Zool. Soc. 1873, p. 146, pl. 15, fig. 4; Thes. Conch. vol. v. pl. 512, fig. 720.—Agulhas Bank.

CONUS GRADATULUS, *Weinkauff*, Thes. Conch. vol. v. pl. 508, fig. 673 = *Conus turritus*, Sowerby, Proc. Zool. Soc. 1870, p. 256, pl. 22, fig. 14.—Agulhas Bank.

STROMBUS FLORIDUS, *Lamk.*, Reeve, Conch. Icon. sp. 11. = *S. mutabilis* (Swainson), Sowerby, Thes. Conch.—Natal coast (Krauss), Port Elizabeth (Crawford). Common and widely distributed in the Indian and Indo-Pacific Oceans.

STROMBUS MAURITIANUS, *Lamarck*, Reeve, Conch. Icon. sp. 20. = *S. cylindricus* (Swainson), Sowb. Thes. Conch. vol. i. pl. 7, fig. 50.—Cape (Dunker).

STROMBUS GIBBERULUS, *Linn.*, Reeve, Conch. Icon. sp. 15; Sowb. Thes. Conch. vol. i. pl. 6, fig. 18.—Natal coast

(Krauss). Very common in the Red Sea and on many Indian and Indo-Pacific coasts. I have not met with it among South African shells.

CYPRÆA CAPENSIS, *Gray*, Thes. Conch. vol. iv. pl. 320, fig. 306.—Port Elizabeth. Confined to the South-African coast.

CYPRÆA EDENTULA, *Sowerby*, Conch. Illustr. No. 102, fig. 26; Thes. Conch. vol. iv. pl. 320, figs. 313, 314.—Port Elizabeth. Confined to the South African coast.

CYPRÆA ALGOENSIS, *Gray*, Sowerby, Conch. Illust. No. 101, fig. 26; Thes. Conch. vol. iv. pl. 320, figs. 311, 312. - This species is very rare in Algoa Bay.

CYPRÆA SIMILIS, *Gray*, Sowerby, Conch. Illust. No. 103, fig. 27; Thes. Conch. vol. iv. pl. 320, figs. 300, 301. Var. *C. castanea* (Higgins), Thes. Conch. vol. iv. pl. 320, figs. 302, 303.—I have only seen one specimen in perfect condition of this species, but bleached ones turn up occasionally. I am convinced that *C. castanea* (Higgins) is the same species.

CYPRÆA AMPHITHALES, *Melvill*, Mem. Manchester Lit. and Phil. Soc. 1888, Ser. 4, vol. i. p. 221, pl. 2, fig. 19.—Port Elizabeth (very rare).

CYPRÆA FUSCO-DENTATA, *Gray*, Sowerby, Conch. Illust. No. 103, fig. 27; Thes. Conch. vol. iv. pl. 320, figs. 298, 299. —Worn specimens are not uncommon at Port Elizabeth, but the shell is seldom found perfect.

CYPRÆA CRUENTA, *Gmelin*, Thes. Conch. vol. iv. pl. 314, fig. 385. = *C. variolaria* (Lamarck).—This species, common on the coast of Mauritius, and on various Indian and Indo-Pacific shores, has, as far as I know, only been found dead at Port Elizabeth.

CYPRÆA CAPUT-SERPENTIS, *Linn.*, Thes. Conch. vol. iv. pl. 304, figs. 72, 73. This very common species is but rarely found on the South-African coast.

CYPRÆA FIMBRIATA, *Gmelin*, Thes. Conch. vol. iv. pl. 323, figs. 390, 391.—Natal coast (Krauss), Port Elizabeth (Bairstow). Widely distributed from Mauritius to the Sandwich Islands, Japan, Borneo, and Australia.

CYPRÆA FELINA, *Gmelin*. Thes. Conch. vol. iv. pl. 323, fig. 393.—Natal coast (Krauss), Port Elizabeth (Bairstow). Distribution about the same as the last.

CYPRÆA CITRINA, *Gray*, Thes. Conch. vol. iv. pl. 316, figs. 218, 219.—This species has been confounded with *C. helvola*, from which it is quite distinct. South Africa and Madagascar (rare).

CYPRÆA HELVOLA, *Linn.*, Thes. Conch. vol. iv. pl. 316, fig. 214.—Port Elizabeth (Bairstow), Natal coast (Krauss). Very common on various Indian and Indo-Pacific shores.

CYPRÆA ARABICA, *Linn.*, Thes. Conch. vol. iv. pl. 302, fig. 61.—Port Elizabeth (Bairstow), Natal coast (Krauss). Common and widely distributed in the Indian and Pacific Oceans.

CYPRÆA ANNULUS, *Linn.*, Thes. Conch. vol. iv. pl. 317, figs. 252, 253.—Natal coast (Krauss), Port Elizabeth (Bairstow). Distribution same as last.

CYPRÆA NEGLECTA, *Sowerby*, Thes. Conch. vol. iv. pl. 323, fig. 377.—Port Elizabeth (Bairstow). Distribution same as last.

CYPRÆA EROSA, *Linn.*, Thes. Conch. vol. iv. pl. 309, fig. 111. Natal coast (Krauss), Port Elizabeth (Bairstow). Distribution same as last.

CYPRÆA CARNEOLA, *Linn.*, Thes. Conch. vol. iv. pl. 294, fig. 11.—Port Elizabeth (Bairstow). Distribution same as last.

CYPRÆA CAURICA, *Linn.*, Thes. Conch. vol. iv. pl. 311, figs. 288, 289.—A dead specimen found at Port Elizabeth.

CYPRÆA MAURITIANA, *Linn.*, Thes. Conch. vol. iv. pl. 301, fig. 51.—Port Elizabeth (Bairstow). Although this species is not confined to the Mauritian coast, but pretty widely distributed in the Indian Ocean, it is not common on the South African coast.

CYPRÆA LAMARCKII, *Gray*, Thes. Conch. vol. iv. pl. 308, fig. 105. =*C. miliaris*, Kiener (non Linn.).—Natal Bay (Krauss), Port Elizabeth (Bairstow), Madagascar, and various parts of the Indian Ocean.

CYPRÆA ISABELLA, *Linn.*, Thes. Conch. vol. iv. pl. 295, fig. 16.—Port Elizabeth (Bairstow). Common on various Indian and Indo-Pacific shores.

CYPRÆA OCELLATA, *Linn.*, Thes. Conch. vol. iv. pl. 108, figs. 102, 103.—Port Elizabeth (Bairstow). Common in the Indian Ocean.

CYPRÆA MONETA, *Linn.*, Thes. Conch. vol. iv. pl. 317, fig. 244.—Port Elizabeth (Bairstow). Very abundant on various shores from Zanzibar to Polynesia.

CYPRÆA TABESCENS, *Solander*, Thes. Conch. vol. iv. pl. 318, fig. 261.—Port Elizabeth (Bairstow). A dead specimen. Common in Mauritius and in various parts of the Indian Ocean.

CYPRÆA ZICZAC, *Linn.*, Thes. Conch. vol. iv. pl. 310, fig. 135.—Port Elizabeth (Bairstow). Common and widely distributed in the Indian and Pacific Oceans.

CYPRÆA STAPHYLÆA, *Linn.*, Thes. Conch. vol. iv. pl. 316, figs. 223, 227.—Port Elizabeth (Bairstow). Common and widely distributed in the Indian and Pacific Oceans.

CYPRÆA LYNX, *Lamarck*, Thes. Conch. vol. iv. pl. 306, fig. 86*.--Natal coast (Krauss). Very common on various Indian and Pacific shores.

CYPRÆA VITELLUS, *Lamarck*, Thes. Conch. vol. iv. pl. 297, fig. 33.—Natal coast (Krauss), Port Elizabeth (Bairstow). Very common on various Indian and Pacific shores.

CYPRÆA UNDATA, *Lamarck*, Thes. Conch. vol. iv. pl. 310, figs. 131-133.—Natal coast (Krauss). Common on various Indian and Pacific shores.

CYPRÆA NEBULOSA, *Kiener*, Coq. Viv. p. 63, pl. 32, fig. 3 ; Sowerby, Thes. Conch. vol. iv. pl. 314, fig. 198.—'Cape' (Kiener). I have never met with this species excepting from West Africa (Gambia).

CYPRÆA LISTERI, *Gray*, Thes. Conch. vol. iv. pl. 309, figs. 116, 117.—Natal coast (Krauss). Sparingly distributed among the Pacific islands. I have never met with this species from South Africa.

F

CYPRÆA (TRIVIA) ONISCUS, *Lamarck*, Thes. Conch. vol. iv. pl. 324, figs. 416, 417. A smooth-backed variety of this species has often been mistaken for *C. ovula*, from which it is constantly distinguished by being when adult ribbed at the base.—Port Elizabeth and Cape coast.

CYPRÆA (TRIVIA) OVULA, *Lamk.*, Thes. Conch. vol. iv. pl. 324, figs. 410, 411.—Port Elizabeth and Cape coast.

CYPRÆA (TRIVIA) COSTATA, *Gmelin*, Thes. Conch. vol. iv. pl. 324, figs. 414, 415 = *C. rosea*, Wood = *C. carnea*, Gray; Sowb. Conch. Illustr. fig. 147.— Cape coast, very rare (Krauss). I have not met with this species from Port Elizabeth.

CYPRÆA (TRIVIA) FORMOSA, *Gaskoin*, Thes. Conch. vol. iv. pl. 328, figs. 518*, 519.— Cape coast and Port Elizabeth.

CYPRÆA (TRIVIA) PELLUCIDULA, *Gaskoin*, Thes. Conch. vol. iv. pl. 327, figs. 497–499. Port Elizabeth.

CYPRÆA (TRIVIA) VESICULARIS, *Gaskoin*, Thes. Conch. vol. iv. pl. 324, figs. 412, 413.—Port Elizabeth. Rarely found in good condition. This species is like a miniature *C. oniscus*, but more finely ribbed.

OVULA SPELTA, *Linn.*, Thes. Conch. vol. i. pl. 100, figs. 63, 64.—Port Elizabeth, Cape coast. Known as a Mediterranean species.

OVULA BIROSTRIS, *Linn.*, Sowerby, Thes. Conch. vol. i. pl. 100, figs. 65, 66.—Port Elizabeth. Of wide distribution. Specimens have been found at Mauritius, Ceylon, Singapore, Hong Kong, Japan, &c.

OVULA CARNEA, *Poiret*, Thes. Conch. vol. i. pl. 101, fig. 77.— A large, light variety of this common Mediterranean species found at Port Elizabeth.

OVULA AURANTIA, *Sowerby*, pl. 1, fig. 26; Journ. of Conch. 1889, vol. vi. p. 11, pl. 1, fig. 15.—Port Elizabeth (Bairstow).

CANCELLARIA FOVEOLATA, *Sowerby*, Thes. Conch. vol. i. pl. 93, figs. 30, 31.—Port Elizabeth. The species varies in colour from nearly white to dark brown or nearly black.

CANCELLARIA SEMIDISJUNCTA, *Sowerby*, Thes. Conch. vol. i. pl. 95, figs. 62, 63.—Port Elizabeth.

CANCELLARIA LAMELLOSA, *Hinds*, Zool. of Voyage of Sulphur, p. 43, pl. 12, figs. 15. 16.—Agulhas Bank, 70 fathoms (Hinds).

CERITHIUM VULGATUM, *Linn.*, Thes. Conch. vol. ii. pl. 179, fig. 67.—A small pale variety of this common Mediterranean species found at Port Elizabeth.

CERITHIUM TUBERCULATUM, *Linn.*, Thes. Conch. vol. ii. pl. 182, fig. 164.—Natal (Crawford).

CERITHIUM COLUMNA, *Sowerby*, Thes. Conch. vol. ii. pl. 178, fig. 56.—Natal (Crawford).

CERITHIUM TÆNIATUM, *Sowerby*, Thes. Conch. vol. iii. pl. 290, fig. 320.—Natal.

CERITHIUM CONTRACTUM, *Sowerby*, Thes. Conch. vol. ii. pl. 184, fig. 218.—Natal.

CERITHIUM PINGUE, *A. Adams*, Thes. Conch. vol. ii. pl. 148, fig. 217.—Port Elizabeth.

CERITHIUM MEDITERRANEUM, *Deshayes*, Thes. Conch. vol. ii. pl. 181, figs. 131, 132.—Port Elizabeth. Common in the Mediterranean, and a variety is found on the Mauritian coast.

CERITHIUM KOCHII, *Philippi*, Thes. Conch. vol. ii. pl. 176, figs. 13-15.—Port Elizabeth (rare), Red Sea, Indian Ocean, Mauritius, China Sea, &c. (common).

CERITHIUM (VERTAGUS) OBELISCUS, *Bruguière*, Thes. Conch. vol. i. pl. 177, fig. 30.—Natal coast (Krauss). Common in the Indian Ocean.

CERITHIUM ECHINATUM, *Lamarck*, Thes. Conch. vol. ii. pl. 178, fig. 44.—Natal Bay (Krauss). Common on many coasts, from Mauritius to the Philippines.

CERITHIUM MONILIFERUM, *Dufresne*, Thes. Conch. vol. ii. pl. 182, fig. 163.—Natal coast (Krauss), Red Sea, Philippines, South Sea Islands, &c.

CERITHIUM FOVEOLATUM, *Sowerby*, nov. sp., pl. 1, fig. 27.
- Testa minima, acuminata, sordide albida; spira acuminata; anfractus 10, leviter convexi, sutura leviter impressa sejuncti, cancellati, profunde seriatim foveolati; anfractus ultimus curtus, ad basin leviter contractus; apertura breviter expansa; columella leviter contorta.

Long. 4 millim.

Hab. Port Elizabeth.

A little dull white species, the surface of which is deeply punctured.

CERITHIDEA DECOLLATA, *Linn.*, Thes. Conch. vol. ii. pl. 186, fig. 276. –Port Elizabeth (Crawford), Natal (Krauss), Zanzibar, Madagascar, Mauritius, &c.

TRIFORIS CARTERETENSIS, *Hinds*, Zool. Voy. Sulphur, Moll. p. 29, pl. 8, fig. 17. – Natal coast (Krauss).

TRIFORIS PERVERSUS, *Linn.*, Sowb. Ill. Index Brit. Shells, pl. 15, fig. 10.—Port Elizabeth (Crawford). This well-known European species is of very wide distribution.

TRIFORIS CINGULATUS, *A. Adams*, Proc. Zool. Soc. 1851, p. 279.—Cape of Good Hope.

LITTORINA KNYSNAENSIS, *Krauss*, Philippi, Conch. vol. xi. p. 196, pl. 4, fig. 4.—Port Elizabeth. This is a variable species and includes *L. africana*, Krauss.

LITTORINA NATALENSIS, *Krauss*, Philippi, Abbild. u. Beschr. n. Conch. vol. ii. p. 160, pl. 3, fig. 4.—Algoa Bay and Natal coast (Krauss).

LITTORINA DECOLLATA, *Krauss*, Phil. Conch. vol. ii. p. 196, pl. 4, fig. 3.—Natal coast (Krauss).

LITTORINA AHENEA, *Reeve*, Conch. Icon. sp. 15.—Port Elizabeth. Of very wide distribution in the Atlantic, Pacific, and Indian Oceans.

LITTORINA ZIGZAC, *Chemnitz*, Reeve, Conch. Icon. sp. 57. —Natal coast (Crawford).

LITTORINA ASPERA, *Philippi*, Proc. Zool. Soc. 1845, p. 139; Tryon, Man. of Conch. vol. ix. pl. 44, figs. 80-85 &c.

LITTORINA NEWCOMBI, *Reeve*, Conch. Icon. sp. 28.—Natal (Crawford).

LITTORINA INTERMEDIA, *Philippi*, Reeve, Conch. Icon. sp. 101.—Natal Bay (Krauss), Borneo, Philippines, &c.

LITTORINA PUNCTATA, *Gmelin*, Reeve, Conch. Icon. sp. 66. —Cape coast (Dunker), Senegal, &c.

LITTORINA GLABRATA, *Philippi*, Reeve, Conch. Icon. sp. 104.—Natal coast (Krauss).

PLANAXIS SULCATUS, *Quoy et Gaimard*, Reeve, Conch. Icon. sp. 24.—Natal coast (Krauss). Common on various coasts in the Indian and Pacific Oceans.

PLANAXIS ACUTUS, *Krauss*, Sudafr. Moll. p. 103, pl. 6, fig. 2.—Natal (Krauss).

MIRALDA CRISPA, *Sowerby*, n. sp., pl. 2, fig. 55.—Testa elongato-pyramidata, alba, nitens; spira acuta, turrita; sutura canaliculata; anfractus 6-7, medio leviter angulati, tricarinati, carinis acute nodulosis, interstitiis plicatis; anfractus ultimus inferne rotundatus, vix protractus; apertura ovata; columella leviter contorta, plica unica acuta minutissima superne instructa.
Long. 3, diam. maj. 1 millim.
Hab. Port Elizabeth.
A little silvery shell, crisply noduled.

AURICULINA LUCIDA, *Sowerby*, n. sp., pl. 2, fig. 39.—Testa elongata, alba, polita, subpellucida; apice obtusa; anfractus 6, leviter convexi; anfractus ultimus oblongus; apertura antice latiuscula, postice acute attenuata; columella leviter contorta; peristoma simplex.
Long. 4, diam. maj. 1 millim.
Hab. Port Elizabeth.
A small white pellucid shell of simple character.

RISSOINA ELEGANTULA, *Angas*, P. Z. S. 1880, p. 417, pl. 40, fig. 10.—Port Elizabeth (Crawford).

RISSOA (ALVANIA) FENESTRATA, *Krauss*, Sudafr. Moll. p. 86, pl. 5, fig. 20.—Port Elizabeth.

RISSOA PINNÆ, *Krauss*, Sudafr. Moll. p. 87, pl. 5, fig. 21. —Port Elizabeth.

RISSOA NIGRA, *Krauss*, Sudafr. Moll. p. 86, pl. 5, fig. 19. —Algoa Bay and Table Bay (Krauss).

RISSOA (ALVANIA) ARGENTEA, *Sowerby*, nov. sp., pl. 11, fig. 40.—Testa acuminato-ovata, imperforata, argenteo-nitens, pellucida ; spira acutiuscula, gradata ; anfractus 6, convexi, liris approximatis, leviter granulatis (in anfr. penult. 4–5, in anfr. ult. circ. 8), sculpti, superne longitudinaliter plicati ; anfractus ultimus leviter inflatus ; apertura ovata ; peristoma simplex ; columella arcuata.

Long. 2, diam. maj. 1¼ mill.

Hab. Port Elizabeth.

A beautiful little shining silvery shell, not regularly latticed like *R. fenestrata*, but with the spiral ridges much more prominent than the longitudinal plaits, which are numerous and visible only on the upper half of the whorls.

RISSOA (CINGULA) CAPENSIS, *Sowerby*, nov. sp., pl. 2, fig. 41.—Testa ovata, anguste perforata, fulvo-cornea, zona lata fusca cincta ; spira breviter turrita, acutiuscula, sutura profunda ; anfractus 5½, laeves, convexi ; anfractus ultimus spiram paulo superans, leviter inflatus ; apertura ovata, infra angulata ; peristoma simplex.

Long. 2, diam. maj. 1¼ millim.

Hab. Port Elizabeth.

A smooth horny umbilicated species with a single broad brown band.

CÆCUM GLABRUM, *Montagu*, Sowb. Ill. Index Brit. Shells, pl. 15, fig. 7.—Port Elizabeth.

TURRITELLA CARINIFERA, *Lamarck*, Reeve, Conch. Icon. sp. 12—Natal, Table Bay and Port Elizabeth.

TURRITELLA BACILLUM, *Kiener*, Reeve, Conch. Icon. sp. 7. —Natal Bay (Krauss). This species is widely distributed in the Indian and Pacific Oceans. I have not met with it among South African shells.

TURRITELLA CAPENSIS, *Krauss*, Sudafr. Moll. p. 106, pl. 6, fig. 8. -Table Bay (Krauss).

TURRITELLA KNYSNAËNSIS, *Krauss*, Sudafr. Moll. p. 106, pl. 6, fig. 9 ; Knysna (Krauss).—Port Elizabeth (Crawford).

TURRITELLA EXCAVATA, *Sowerby*, Proc. Zool. Soc. 1870, p. 252, pl. 21, fig. 3.—Aghulhas Bank.

TURRITELLA PUNCTULATA, *Sowerby*, Proc. Zool. Soc. 1870, p. 253.—Agulhas Bank.

VERMETUS (SIPHONIUM) NEBULOSUS, *Dillwyn*, Tryon, vol. viii. p. 184, pl. 54, figs. 84–86.

VERMETUS (THYLACODES) CONICUS, *Dillwyn*, Tryon, vol. viii. pl. 49, fig. 24. = *V. decussatus* (Gmelin).—Port Elizabeth.

VERMETUS (STREPHOPOMA) TRICUSPE, *Mörch.*, P. Z. S. 1861, p. 150.—South Africa.

SILIQUARIA OBTUSA, *Schumacher*, Sowerby, Thes. Conch. vol. v. pl. 480, fig. 3. = *S. anguina*, Philippi, *non* Linn.— Only small specimens of this species have been found at Port Elizabeth. Distribution: Mediterranean, Senegal, &c.

TROCHITA HELICOIDEA, *Sowerby*, Thes. Conch. vol. v. pl. 449, figs. 53, 54.—Port Elizabeth (Bairstow).

TROCHITA CHINENSIS, *Linn.*, Sowerby, Illust. Index Brit. Shells, pl. 10, fig. 29.—Port Elizabeth. The South-African specimens of this European species are mostly purple-tinted.

CREPIDULA ASPERSA, *Dunker*, Thes. Conch. vol. v. pl. 452, figs. 126, 127.—Port Elizabeth; Lower Guinea (Dunker). This appears to be a young shell. I am not sure that *C. lentiginosa* is not the adult form of this species.

CREPIDULA RUGULOSA, *Dunker*, Zeitsch. für Malakozool. 1846, p. 108.—Table Bay (Krauss).

CREPIDULA ACULEATA, *Gmelin*, Thes. Conch. vol. v. pl. 452, fig. 124.—Table Bay, Simon's Bay, Natal coast, Port Elizabeth; also found on the Atlantic coast of South America; and a variety (*costata*) inhabits the shore of Nagasaki, Japan (Lischke).

CREPIDULA HEPATICA, *Deshayes*, Thes. Conch. vol. v. pl. 453, figs. 131, 132.—Table Bay, Natal, Port Elizabeth, &c.

CREPIDULA LENTIGINOSA, *Sowerby*, Thes. Conch. vol. v. pl. 453, fig. 130.—Port Elizabeth. Possibly the adult form of *C. aspersa* (Dunker).

HIPPONYX PILOSUS, *Deshayes*, Tryon, M. of C., vol. viii. pl. 40, fig. 3.—Natal coast (Krauss).

HIPPONYX GRANULATUS, *A. Adams*, Proc. Zool. Soc. 1853, p. 171, pl. 20, fig. 3.—Natal and Port Elizabeth.

HIPPONYX AUSTRALIS, *Quoy and Gaimard*, Tryon's Manual, vol. viii. p. 136, pl. 41, figs. 12, 13. = *H. aculus* (Quoy).—Natal coast (Krauss).

NERITA ALBICILLA, *Linn.*, Thes. Conch. vol. v. p. 464, figs. 26, 27.—Natal coast (Krauss), Port Elizabeth (Bairstow and Crawford), Mauritius, Red Sea, &c.

NERITA POLITA, *Linn.*, Thes. Conch. vol. v. pl. 463, figs. 2, 3.—Natal coast (Krauss), Port Elizabeth, Zanzibar, Mauritius, &c.

NERITA UMLASSIANA, *Krauss*, Sudafr. Moll. p. 89, pl. 5, fig. 25.—Mouth of River Knysna (Krauss).

NERITA QUADRICOLOR, *Gmelin*, Thes. Conch. vol. v. pl. 463, fig. 14. Natal Point (Krauss). This species is common in the Red Sea. I have not met with it from South Africa.

NERITA PLICATA, *Linn.*, Thes. Conch., vol. v. pl. 466, figs. 79, 80. — Very common on various parts of the South African coast.

NERITA EXUVIA, *Linn.*, Thes. Conch. vol. v. pl. 464, fig. 34. Natal Bay (Krauss). I have not met with this species from South Africa. It is common in various parts of the Indian Ocean.

NERITA PLEXA, *Chemnitz*, Thes. Conch. vol. v. pl. 464, fig. 33.—Port Elizabeth. Widely distributed in the Indian Ocean.

NERITA SANGUINOLENTA, *Menke*, Thes. Conch. vol. v. pl. 468, fig. 113 (as *albicilla* var). – Port Elizabeth. Distribution: Mauritius, Madagascar, &c.

NERITA COMMA-NOTATA, *Reeve*, Conch. Icon. sp. 72; Thes. Conch. vol. v. pl. 466, fig. 59.

NERITA LISTERI, *Récluz*, Thes. Conch. vol. v. pl. 465, fig. 51.—Port Elizabeth.

PHASIANELLA CAPENSIS, *Dunker*, Krauss, Sudafr. Moll. p. 104, pl. 6, fig. 5.—Port Elizabeth, Simon's Bay, Table Bay, &c.

PHASIANELLA KOCHII, *Philippi*, Krauss, Sudafr. Moll. p. 104, pl. 6, fig. 4.—Port Elizabeth, Simon's Bay, Table Bay, &c.

PHASIANELLA ELONGATA, *Krauss*, Sudafr. Moll. p. 104, pl. 6, fig. 3.—Cape (Krauss), Port Elizabeth, &c.

PHASIANELLA PULLUS, var. *P. tennis* (Philippi), Sowerby, Thes. Conch. vol. v. pl. 476, fig. 30.—Cape coast (Krauss).

PHASIANELLA BICARINATA, *Dunker*, Tryon, vol. x. p. 176, pl. 39a, fig. 10.—Cape (Dunker). I am not acquainted with this species. It has an abnormal look.

PHASIANELLA NERITINA, *Dunker*, Krauss, Sudafr. Moll. p. 105, pl. 6, fig. 6 ; Thes. Conch. vol. v. pl. 476, fig. 10. — Cape (Krauss).

TURBO CORONATUS, *Gmelin*, Thes. Conch. vol. v. pl. 498, fig. 51.—Natal coast (Krauss). Distribution : Red Sea to the East Indian Archipelago.

TURBO SARMATICUS, *Linn.*, Thes. Conch. vol. v. pl. 497, fig. 43. = *classiarius* (Gray).—Port Elizabeth and various parts of the South African coast.

TURBO CIDARIS, *Gmelin*, Thes. Conch. vol. v. pl. 496, fig. 35, var. *C. natalensis* (*Reeve*), Conch. Icon. (Turbo) sp. 1 ; Thes. Conch. vol. v. pl. 497, fig. 41. *Turbo natalensis* has not only been considered specifically distinct from *T. cidaris*, but it has been placed in a different genus on account of the curiously tufted granulation of the operculum. After comparison of a large number of specimens, Mr. Ponsonby, Professor Gwatkin, and I have come to the conclusion that it is a mere variety. The shells vary a good deal, from a strongly-ribbed growth to perfectly smooth, also in the height of the spire, &c., but they cannot be separated by any reliable character. In the operculum the size of the granulation and more or less perforated centre seem to vary indiscriminately. Then, as to the animal, Mr. Gwatkin says : ' A careful examination of *T. cidaris* and *natalensis* leaves me at a loss for any clear difference of dentition. The

G

specimens vary a little, but only a little, and that promiscu-
ously. I cannot find any specific difference.'

TURBO (COLLONIA) SANGUINEUS, *Linn.*, Sowerby, Thes.
Conch. vol. v. pl. 504, fig. 146. = *T. quantilla* (Gould).—Port
Elizabeth (Crawford), Mediterranean, Vancouver Island, &c.

TURBO (COLLONIA) MINUTUS, *Sowerby*, pl. 2, fig. 53 ; J. of
C. 1889, vol. vi. p. 152, pl. 3, fig. 9.—Port Elizabeth. Since
describing this species I have seen a couple of specimens of
rather larger size.

OXYSTELE MERULA, *Lamarck*, Tryon, vol. xi. pl. 23, fig 79.
—Port Elizabeth (plentiful).

OXYSTELE TIGRINUS, *Chemnitz*, Tryon, vol. xi. pl. 23,
figs. 61-64.—Port Elizabeth (plentiful).

OXYSTELE NIGER, *A. Adams* (*Photinula*), P. Z. S. 1851,
p. 192.—Port Elizabeth.

OXYSTELE ZONATUS, *Wood*, Tryon, vol. xi. p. 238, pl. 36,
fig. 21 (as Gibbula).—Port Elizabeth, Simon's Bay, &c.

OXYSTELE IMPERVIUS, *Menke*, Philippi, Conch. Cab. p. 145,
pl. 24, fig. 8 ; var. *Trochus sagittiferus* (Lamarck), Phil.
Conch. Cab. pl. 24. fig. 16 ; var. *Trochus indecorus*, Phil.
Conch. Cab. p. 143, pl. 24, fig. 5 ; var. *Trochus variegatus*
(Anton).—Agulhas Bank (Krauss), Simon's Bay, Table Bay,
Port Elizabeth, &c. (common).

OXYSTELE TABULARIS, *Krauss*, Sudafr. Moll. p. 97, pl. 5,
fig. 30.—Table Bay (Krauss), Natal and Port Elizabeth.

OXYSTELE TAMSI, *Dunker*, Index Moll. Guinea, p. 16,
pl. 2, figs. 40-42.—Cape (Dunker), Guinea, Cape de Verde
Islands, &c.

CALLIOSTOMA ORNATUM, *Lamarck* (*Trochus*), Reeve,
Conch. Icon. (Ziziphinus), sp. 7.—Several varieties of this
pretty shell found at Port Elizabeth.

CALLIOSTOMA EUGLYPTUS, *A. Adams*, Reeve, Conch. Icon.
(Ziziphinus), sp. 17.—Port Elizabeth (rare). Reputed habi-
tats : Australia, Tasmania, &c.

CALLIOSTOMA BICINGULATUM, *Lamarck* (Trochus), Reeve,
Conch. Icon. (Ziziphinus), sp. 20. Cape coast (Krauss).
This species is quoted from Torres Straits.

CALLIOSTOMA FULTONI, *Sowerby*, pl. 2, fig. 43; Journal of Conchology, 1889, vol. vi. p. 153, pl. 3, fig. 7.—Port Elizabeth.

CALLIOSTOMA FARQUHARI, *Sowerby*, nov. sp., pl. 2, fig. 42.
—Testa conica, elata, angustissime umbilicata, grisea, fusco-maculata; spira lævissime convexa, ad apicem acuta; anfractus 7-8, planato-declives, spiraliter dense lirati, oblique subtilissime striati, inferne angulati, ad angulum maculis fuscis ornati; basis convexa, liris circ. 12, exsculpta; apertura leviter obliqua, fauce lævi; columella rectiuscula, leviter callosa; peristoma acutum.
Long. 12; diam. maj. 9 millim.
Hab. Port Elizabeth.
This species is not far removed from *C. Fultoni*, from which it is chiefly distinguished by its strong spiral sculpture, and by the row of brown spots at the angle.

GIBBULA GRANULOSA, *Dunker* (*Delphinula*), Krauss, Sudafr. Moll. p. 94, pl. 5, fig. 28.—Table Bay (Krauss), Simon's Bay and Port Elizabeth.

GIBBULA CAPENSIS, *Gmelin*, Philippi, Conch. Cab. pl. 29, fig. 22.—Port Elizabeth, Natal, &c.

GIBBULA ROSEA, *Gmelin*. See Journal of Conch., 1889, vol. vi. p. 153.

GIBBULA MULTICOLOR, *Krauss*, Sudafr. Moll. p. 97, pl. 5, fig. 31.—Table Bay (Krauss), Port Elizabeth (Crawford).

GIBBULA ZEYHERI, *Krauss*, Archiv für Nat. 1852, p. 33.
—I do not know this species, but from the description it appears to be nearly allied to *G. cicer*.

GIBBULA ARMILLATA, *A. Adams* (MSS.?), Sowerby (Turbo), Thes. Conch. vol. v. pl. 50, fig. 93.—Port Elizabeth. Having examined the operculum of this little shell, I find it to belong to the genus *Gibbula*, and not to *Collonia* as the form of the shell led me to suppose.

GIBBULA CICER, *Menke*. See Journal of Conch. 1889, vol. vi. p. 153. *Turbo cicer* (Sowerby), Thes. Conch. vol. v. pl. 505, fig. 59. This is the *Trochus musivus* of Gould.—Table Bay, Simon's Bay, and Port Elizabeth.

GIBBULA BENZI, *Krauss*, Sudafr. Moll. p. 99, pl. 5, fig. 32.
Port Elizabeth.

GIBBULA LUDWIGI, *Krauss*, Sudafr. Moll. p. 99, pl. 5,
fig. 33.—Cape (Krauss). Unknown to me.

GIBBULA MINIATA, *Anton*, Philippi, Beschr. und Abbild.
vol. i. p. 33, pl. 1. fig. 7.—Table Bay (Krauss). Unknown
to me.

GIBBULA PONSONBYI, *Sowerby*, Proc. Zool. Soc. 1888;
Journal of Conchology, 1889, vol. v. p. 11.—Port Elizabeth.

GIBBULA BIPORCATA, *A. Adams* (MSS.?).—Port Elizabeth
(rare). See Addendum.

TROCHUS (POLYDONTA) NIGROPUNCTATUS, *Reeve*, Conch.
Icon. (Trochus), sp. 71.—Port Elizabeth (a young shell).

SOLARIELLA FUSCO-MACULATA, *Sowerby*, nov. sp., pl. 11,
fig. 46.—Testa minuta, late et profunde umbilicata, depresse
orbicularis, lævis, albida, maculis parvis fuscis irregulariter
conspersis picta; spira obtusa, vix elevata; anfractus 4½,
convexi; sutura anguste canaliculata sejuncti; anfr. ultimus depresse rotundatus; basis radiatim plicata; umbilicus
perspectivus. Apertura circularis, parviuscula; peristoma
simplex.
Diam. 3½; alt. 2½ millim.
Hab. Port Elizabeth.
A pretty little species, of which Mr. Ponsonby has shown
me one fresh specimen, and several dead ones. One or two
of the dead ones are a little larger than the type. The shell
is quite smooth, excepting the puckering of the base, com-
mencing in the umbilicus.

SOLARIELLA DILECTA, *A. Adams* (pl. 4, fig. 90), Proc.
Zool. Soc. 1854, p. 40 (Margarita); Journal of Conch. 1889,
vol. vi. p. 154.—Port Elizabeth. The type in the Cumingian
collection is labelled 'Straits of Magellan.'

SOLARIELLA UNDATA, *Sowerby*, Proc. Zool. Soc. 1870,
p. 251.—Agulhas Bank.

MONODONTA AUSTRALIS, *Deshayes*, Tryon, Manual, vol. xi.
p. 88, pl. 62, fig. 84.—Natal (Krauss).

MONODONTA (PRIOTROCHUS) OBSCURA, *Wood*, Tryon, vol. xi. p. 257, pl. 61, fig. 33.—Natal (Crawford).

CLANCULUS CARINATUS, *A. Adams*, Proc. Zool. Soc. 1851, p. 162; Tryon, vol. xi. pl. 14, fig. 24-26.—Port Elizabeth.

CLANCULUS PUNICEUS, *Philippi*, Conch. Cab. p. 73, pl. 14, fig. 2.—Natal coast (Krauss). Distribution: Red Sea, Zanzibar, Senegal, &c. I have not met with this species among South African shells; it is nearly allied to, if not a mere variety of *C. Pharaonis*.

CLANCULUS LACEYI, *Sowerby*, pl. 11, fig. 44; Journal of Conch. 1889, vol. vi. p. 11, pl. 1, fig. 16.—Port Elizabeth.

CLANCULUS WALTONÆ, *Sowerby*, n. sp., pl. 2, fig. 45. —Testa breviter conica, fuscescens, maculis minutis nigrofuscis irregulariter aspersa; anfractus 5½, convexiusculi, liris spiralibus granulatis (in aufr. penult. 4. lira minima interveniente) ornati, sutura canaliculata sejuncti; anfractus ultimus obtuse angulatus; basis leviter convexa, liris granulatis circ. 9 ornata; umbilicus profunde excavatus; columella obliqua, supra et infra angulata; apertura leviter obliqua, subquadrata, fauce iridescens.

Diam. 11; alt. 8¼ millim.

Hab. Port Elizabeth (Crawford).

Somewhat resembling *C. carinatus* and *C. Laceyi*, with the ridges crisply granulated. In form it is more elevated and inflated than *C. carinatus*.

CYCLOSTREMA ROTUNDATA, *Sowerby*, n. sp., pl. 2, fig. 47. —Testa orbiculata, anguste umbilicata, albida, subpellucida; spira obtusa, sutura canaliculata; anfractus 4, convexi, spiraliter striati; anfractus ultimus rotunde convexus: apertura leviter obliqua, subcircularis.

Diam. 2½; alt. 1½ millim.

Hab. Port Elizabeth.

A little white shell, of which the true generic position is uncertain. The species varies a good deal in form, and in the width of the umbilicus, which in some specimens is nearly closed.

CYCLOSTREMA INFLATA, *Sowerby*, n. sp., pl. 11, fig. 48.— Testa inflata, anguste umbilicata, tenuis, alba; spira parva, acutiuscula, gradata; sutura profunda; anfractus 4, primi

biangulati; anfractus ultimus inflatus, rotundatus, sub-
oblique oblongus, spiraliter obscure liratus, minutissime
striatus; apertura subcircularis, leviter obliqua; peristoma
continuum, simplex.

Diam. maj. 9½; alt. 7 mill.

A thin white inflated species, with a narrow umbilicus,
upper whorls bi-angulated, body-whorl very finely striated,
and showing very faint traces of spiral ribs; the spire is very
small and rather acute, and the whorls are divided by a deep
suture.

Hab. Port Elizabeth.

CYCLOSTREMA PLANULATA, *Sowerby*, n. sp., pl. 11, fig. 49.
—Testa orbiculata, compressa, tenuis, alba, late et profunde
umbilicata; spira parva, vix exserta, planulata; anfractus
3½, spiraliter striati; anfractus ultimus planato-convexus,
acutissime carinatus; basis concava, lira elevata circa umbi-
licum munita; apertura patula; peristoma simplex.

Diam. maj. 5, min. 4½; alt. 1½ millim.

A remarkable little shell, in which the spire is very small
in proportion to the body whorl, which is broad, slightly convex at the top, and flattened at the base, with a sharp keel
at the margin. The shell somewhat resembles in form a
miniature *Trochita calyptraeformis*.

Hab. Port Elizabeth.

LIOTIA PULCHERRIMA, *Adams*, Ann. and Mag. Nat. Hist.
vol. vii. 1851, p. 332.—' Cape of Good Hope' (Mus. Cuming.).

HALIOTIS SANGUINEA, *Hanley*, Reeve, Conch. Icon. fig. 17;
Sowerby, Thes. Conch. vol. v. pl. 439, fig. 93.—Table Bay,
Port Elizabeth, and Cape coast generally.

HALIOTIS MIDÆ, *Linn.*, Reeve, Conch. Icon. fig. 16;
Sowerby, Thes. Conch. vol. v. pl. 431, fig. 31. = *H. capensis*
(Dunker).—Port Elizabeth and Cape coast generally.

HALIOTIS PARVA, *Linn.*, Reeve, Conch. Icon. fig. 53;
Sowerby, Thes. Conch. vol. v. pl. 429, fig. 17. = *H.
canaliculata* (Lamarck).—Table Bay and Port Elizabeth.

STOMATELLA SULCIFERA, *Lamarck*, Sowerby, Thes. Conch.
vol. iii. pl. 174, fig. 3.—Natal (Krauss).

STOMATELLA ARTICULATA, *A. Adams*, Thes. Conch. vol. ii.
pl. 174, fig. 2.—I found a small specimen of this species in

the Bairstow collection; it may possibly be the same species as that identified by Krauss as *S. sulcifera*.

STOMATELLA CANCELLATA, *Krauss*, Sudafr. Moll. p. 93, pl. 5, fig. 26; Sowerby, Thes. Conch. vol. iii. pl. 174.—Table Bay, Natal, &c.

FISSURELLA SCUTELLA, *Gray*, Sowerby, Thes. Conch. vol. iii. pl. 244, fig. 207.—Cape coast (Krauss), Torres Straits.

FISSURELLA CALYCULATA, *Sowerby*, Genera of Shells, No. 21, fig. 4; Thes. Conch. vol. iii. pl. 140, fig. 126.—Port Elizabeth and Cape coast generally.

FISSURELLA SIEBOLDI, *Reeve*, Conch. Icon. sp. 102; Sowerby, Conch. Icon. vol. iii. pl. 241, fig. 138.—Port Elizabeth. Known as a Japanese species.

FISSURELLA INCARNATA, *Krauss*, Sudafr. Moll. p. 65, pl. 4, fig. 7.—Table Bay and Natal (Krauss), Port Elizabeth.

FISSURELLA CONOIDES, *Philippi*, Sowerby, Thes. Conch. vol. iii. p. 189, pl. 3, fig. 51.—Cape of Good Hope.

FISSURELLA NATALENSIS, *Krauss*, Sudafr. Moll. p. 66, pl. 4, fig. 8; Sowerby, Thes. Conch. vol. iii. pl. 239, fig. 69. —Natal coast (Krauss), Port Elizabeth, &c.

FISSURELLA CRUCIATA, *Krauss*, Sudafr. Moll. p. 67, pl. 4, fig. 9; Sowerby, Thes. Conch. vol. iii. pl. 143, fig. 191.— Natal coast (Krauss).

FISSURELLA AUSTRALIS, *Krauss*, Sudafr. Moll. p. 67, pl. 4, fig. 10.—Natal coast (Krauss), Port Elizabeth, &c.

FISSURELLA OBTUSA, *Sowerby*, Conch. Illust. p. 7, fig. 59; Thes. Conch. vol. iii. p. 189, pl. 4, fig. 80.—Cape of Good Hope, coll. G. Humphrey (Sowerby).

FISSURELLA CAFFRA, *Gmelin*, Martini, Conch. Cab. vol. i. pl. 2, fig. 95; *Patella caffra*, Gmelin, No. 201, p. 3730.—'Cape' (Martini).

FISSURELLA ELEVATA, *Dunker*, Philippi, Abbild. und Beschreib. neuer Conch. Bd. ii. p. 67, tab. 2, fig. 4.—Cape coast (Dunker).

FISSURELLA MUTABILIS, *Sowerby*, Conch. Illust. figs. 67, 70; Thes. Conch. vol. iii. pl. 239, fig. 70.—Table Bay, Natal coast, and Port Elizabeth.

FISSURELLA NEGLECTA, *Deshayes*, Sowerby, Thes. Conch. vol. iii. pl. 241, fig. 139.—Port Elizabeth. A well-known Mediterranean species.

FISSURELLA NUBECULA, *Linn.*, Sowerby, Thes. Conch. vol. iii. pl. 239, fig. 73.—Port Elizabeth and Mediterranean.

FISSURELLA ROBUSTA, *Sowerby*, pl. 2, figs. 50, 51; Journ. of Conch. 1889, vol. vi. p. 12, pl. 1, figs. 5, 6.—Port Elizabeth (Crawford). A single worn specimen.

FISSURELLA DUBIA, *Reeve*, Conch. Icon. sp. 35; Sowerby, Thes. Conch. vol. iii. pl. 244, fig. 208.—Cape of Good Hope.

FISSURELLA ROTA, *Reeve*, Conch. Icon. sp. 79; Sowerby, Thes. Conch. vol. iii. pl. 239, fig. 72.—Cape of Good Hope.

FISSURELLA PARVI-FORATA, *Sowerby*, pl. 2, figs. 52, 53; Journ. of Conch. vol. vi. 1889, p. 12, pl. 1, fig. 7.—Port Elizabeth.

FISSURELLA FIMBRIATA, *Reeve*, Conch. Icon. sp. 104. Port Elizabeth.

FISSURELLA FUMATA, *Reeve*, Conch. Icon. sp. 63; Sowerby, Thes. Conch. vol. iii. pl. 149, figs. 95-97.—Port Elizabeth. Quoted as West Indian.

FISSURELLIDEA HIANTULA, *Lamarck*, Sowerby, Thes. Conch. vol. iii. pl. 248, figs. 193-195.—Port Elizabeth and Cape coast generally.

FISSURELLIDEA CONCATENATA, *Crosse and Fischer*, J. de C. vol. xiii. p. 41, pl. 3, figs. 1-3.—Port Elizabeth.

PUPILLIA APERTA, *Sowerby* (Fissurella). Tank. Catal. Supp. p. 6; Thes. Conch. vol. iii. pl. 244, fig. 228.—Port Elizabeth. This species is quoted as from Patagonia, but I have only met with it from South Africa.

MACROCHISMA PRODUCTA, *A. Adams*, Sowerby, Thes. Conch. vol. iii. pl. 244, fig. 224.—Port Elizabeth (Bairstow), a dead specimen. An Australian species.

DENTALIUM LESSONI, *Deshayes*, Sowerby, Thes. Conch. vol. iii. pl. 224, fig. 15.—Port Elizabeth (Crawford), dead specimens. A Mediterranean species.

SCUTUM IMBRICATUM, *Quoy et Gaim.* Voy. de
l'Astrolabe, Moll. vol. iii. p. 323, pl. 69, figs. 17, 18.—Natal
coast (Krauss).

HELCION PECTINATUS, *Linn.* (Patella), Syst. Nat. p. 1259 ;
Chenu. Man. Conch. fig. 2814.—Table Bay, Agulhas Bank,
Port Elizabeth, and Cape coast generally (abundant).

GADINIA COSTATA, *Krauss* (Mouretia), Sudafr. Moll.
p. 57, pl. 4, fig. 1.—Cape coast.

GADINIA AFRA, *Gmelin* (Patella), Syst. Nat. p. 3715 ;
Adams, Gen. Rec. Moll. pl. 52, fig. 8a.—Port Elizabeth.

PATELLA VARIABILIS, *Krauss*, Sudafr. Moll. p. 55, pl. 3,
fig. 12.—Natal coast, Port Elizabeth, &c.

PATELLA COCHLEAR, *Born*, Reeve, Conch. Icon. sp. 24.—
Table Bay, Agulhas Bank, and Port Elizabeth.

PATELLA COMPRESSA, *Linn.*, Reeve, Conch. Icon. sp. 13.—
Port Elizabeth and Cape coast generally.

PATELLA ARGENVILLEI, *Krauss*, Sudafr. Moll. p. 49 ;
Reeve, Conch. Icon. sp. 20.—Table Bay (Krauss), Port
Elizabeth, &c.

PATELLA RUSTICA, *Linn.*, Reeve, Conch. Icon. sp. 8.—
Port Elizabeth, &c.

PATELLA PLICATA, *Born*, Reeve, Conch. Icon. sp. 16. I
doubt very much whether this is anything more than a
variety of *P. rustica.*—Port Elizabeth, &c.

PATELLA TABULARIS, *Krauss*, Sudafr. Moll. p. 47, pl. 3,
fig. 8. In my opinion this also is a form of *P. rustica.*
P. oblecta, Krauss, Sudafr. Moll. p. 47, pl. 3, fig. 11, is
simply the young of the same.—Port Elizabeth, &c.

PATELLA GRANATINA, *Linn.*, Reeve, Conch. Icon. sp. 4.—
Cape coast (common).

PATELLA GRANULARIS, *Linn.*, Reeve, Conch. Icon. sp. 31.
P. echinulata, Krauss (Sudafr. Moll. p. 52, pl. 3, sp. 15), is
the young of this species.—Port Elizabeth, &c.

PATELLA UMBELLA, *Gmelin*, Reeve, Conch. Icon. sp. 17.
P. miniata, Born, is the young of this species.—Port
Elizabeth.

H

PATELLA DUNKERI, *Krauss*, Sudafr. Moll. p. 55, pl. 3, fig. 14. –Port Elizabeth, Cape and Natal coasts.

PATELLA EXARATA, *Nuttal*, Reeve, Conch. Icon. sp. 47.––Port Elizabeth (rare). Common in the Sandwich Islands.

PATELLA SAFIANA, *Lamarck*, = *P. conspicua* (Philippi), Reeve, Conch. Icon. sp. 12. Port Elizabeth (rare). This fine species is also found on the Algerian coast.

PATELLA LONGICOSTA, *Lamarck*, Reeve, Conch. Icon. sp. 11.– Port Elizabeth and other parts of the South African coast.

PATELLA OCULUS, *Born*, Sowerby, Conch. Manual, fig. 229; Reeve, Conch. Icon. sp. 2: *P. badia*, Gmelin; *P. fuscescens*, Gmelin (Krauss); *P. Schroeteri*, Krauss, Sudafr. Moll. p. 43.

PATELLA BARBARA, *Linn.*, Krauss, Sudafr. Moll. p. 45.– Table Bay and Agulhas Bank (Krauss). This species is also quoted from Falkland Islands.

PATELLA NIGRO-ALBA, *Blainville* (Krauss, Sudafr. Moll. p. 53), is unknown to me. 'Cape' (Blainv.).

PATELLA MACULATA, *Blainville* (Krauss, Sudafr. Moll. p. 53), is unknown to me. 'Cape' (Blainv.).

PATELLA CAPENSIS, *Gmelin*, Krauss, Sudafr. Moll. p. 53, pl. 3, fig. 13.—Port Elizabeth and Cape coast generally; also coasts of Madagascar, Mauritius, Ceylon, &c.

PATELLA PRUINOSA, *Krauss*, Sudafr. Moll. p. 56, pl. 3, fig. 9; Reeve, Conch. Icon. sp. 109.—Table Bay, Port Elizabeth, &c. (abundant).

CHITON GIGAS, *Chemnitz*, Reeve, Conch. Icon. fig. 65.— Table Bay, Natal, Port Elizabeth, &c.

CHITON TULIPA, *Quoy*, Reeve, Conch. Icon. sp. 18. = *C. cymbiola. Sowerby.* –Table Bay, Natal coast, Port Elizabeth, &c.

CHITON MARGINATUS. *Pennant*, Sowerby, Illust. Index of Brit. Shells, pl. 10, fig. 13.—Port Elizabeth (not uncommon). This is well known and common on the British, Norwegian, North American, and other coasts.

CHITON GARNETI, *Blainville*, Quoy et Gaim. Voy. de l'Astrol. vol. iii. p. 401, pl. 73, figs. 9-14.—Table Bay, Natal coast, Port Elizabeth, &c.

CHITON TEXTILIS, *Gray*, Spicil. Zool. 1, p. 5; Sowerby, Conch. Illust. 61. = *C. solea*. Sowerby, Conch. Illust. = *C. indicus*, Sowerby.—Table Bay, Port Elizabeth, &c.

CHITON WATSONI, *Sowerby*, Conch. Illust. figs. 81, 82, 130. —Table Bay, &c.

CHITON PRUINOSUS, *Gould*, U. S. Exploring Expedition, 1852, p. 316, fig. 419. = *C. pollicaria*, Carp.—Port Elizabeth.

CHITON PERTUSUS, *Reeve*, Conch. Icon. pl. 16, fig. 88.— Simon's Bay (Krauss).

CHITON CASTANEUS, *Wood*, Sowerby, Conch. Illust. figs. 114-116; Reeve, Conch. Icon. fig. 23. Cape of Good Hope.

CHITON WAHLBERGI, *Krauss*, Sudafr. Moll. p. 36, pl. 3, fig. 1.—Table Bay (Krauss).

CHITON CAPENSIS, *Gray*, Spicil. Zool. p. 5; Reeve, Conch. Icon. sp. 151.—Table Bay and Natal coast.

CHITON TIGRINUS, *Krauss*, Sudafr. Moll. p. 38, pl. 3, fig. 5.—False Bay.

CHITON NIGROVIRESCENS, *Blainville*, Krauss, Sudafr. Moll. p. 38.—'Cape' (Blainv.).

CHITON MACGILLIVRAYI, *Carpenter*.—Port Elizabeth.

CHITON ONISCUS, *Krauss*, Sudafr. Moll. p. 39, pl. 3, fig. 4. Natal coast.

CHITON CYANEO-PUNCTATUS, *Krauss*, Sudafr. Moll. p. 40, pl. 3, fig. 2.—Cape coast (Krauss).

CHITON CARMICHAELIS, *Wood*, Index Test. supp. pl. 1, fig. 10; Spicil. Zool. p. 6.—Cape of Good Hope (Wood).

CHITON PUSTULATUS, *Krauss*, Sudafr. Moll. p. 42, pl. 3, fig. 7.—Natal coast (Wahlberg).

ACTÆON ALBUS, *Sowerby* (Tornatella), Proc. Zool. Soc. 1873, p. 720, pl. 49, fig. 6; Journ. of Conch. 1886, vol. v. p. 15.—Port Elizabeth.

ACTÆON (SOLIDULA) SUTURALIS, *A. Adams*, Reeve, Conch. Icon. Tornatella, sp. 9.—Port Elizabeth and Natal (Crawford).

ACTÆON (SOLIDULA) SOLIDULUS, *Linn.* (Voluta), Reeve, Conch. Icon. Tornatella, sp. 3.—Natal.

HYDATINA PHYSIS, *Linn.*, Reeve, Conch. Icon. Hydatina, sp. 2.—Natal coast (Krauss), Port Elizabeth (Bairstow). Common on the Mauritian coast and various parts of the Indian Ocean.

BULLINA ZICZAC, *Muhlfeldt*, Reeve, Conch. Icon. Bullina, sp. 2. = *B. lineata*, Wood; *B. lauta*, Pease.—Port Elizabeth. A widely distributed species found on the coasts of Mauritius, Ceylon, Sandwich Islands, Australia, &c.

CYLICHNA CYLINDRACEA, *Pennant*, Sowerby's Illust. Index Brit. Shells, pl. 20, fig. 4. Port Elizabeth.

CYLICHNA UMBILICATA, *Montague*, Sowerby, Illust. Index Brit. Shells, pl. 20, fig. 9. Port Elizabeth. A well-known British species.

TORNATINA VOLUTA, *Quoy et Gaimard*, Sowb. Thes. Conch. vol. ii. pl. 121, fig. 24. *T. soluta* (by error J. C. vi. p. 13). —This species is found principally in the Pacific Ocean.

VOLVULA ROSTRATA, *A. Adams*, Sowb. Thes. Conch. vol. ii. p. 96, pl. 125, fig. 154. —Port Elizabeth.

LEUCOTINA ELONGATA, *Sowerby*, n. sp., pl. 11, fig. 57.— Testa elongata, alba; spira turrita, levissime convexa; anfractus 8, convexiusculi, sulcis incisis cire. 8 regularibus, angustiusculis, mediocriter profundis, obscure puncturatis, spiraliter sculpti; sutura profunda sejuncti; aufractus ultimus oblongus; apertura oblongo-ovata, parva, columella recta, peristoma simplex.

Long. 13, diam. maj. 3½; apertura longa 3½, lata 2¼ millim. Hab. Port Elizabeth.

A white shell, spirally grooved, of a more elongated form than the known species of the genus.

LEUCOTINA CASTA, *A. Adams* (Monoptygma), Thes. Conch. vol. ii. pl. 172, fig. 22.—Port Elizabeth.

BULLA AMPULLA, *Linn.*—Natal Bay (Krauss), Port Elizabeth (Bairstow). This is a species of very wide distribution and extremely common in many localities. The South African specimens I have seen are small.

HAMINEA NATALENSIS, *Krauss* (Bulla), Sudafr. Moll. p. 71, pl. 4, fig. 14.—Natal (Krauss), Port Elizabeth.

PHILINE APERTA, *Linn.*, Sowerby's Illust. Index. of Brit. Shells, pl. 20, fig. 20.—A common well-known British species.

PHILINE SCHROETERI, *Philippi* (Bulla), Enum. Moll. Sicil. vol. ii. p. 94, pl. 20, fig. 2.—Table Bay (Krauss), Port Elizabeth (Crawford).

OXYNOE PELLUCIDUS, *A. Adams* (Icarus), H. and A. Adams, Gen. Recent Mollusca, vol. ii. p. 31 (Lophocercus). - Port Elizabeth (Crawford).

CYLINDROBULLA FRAGILIS, *Jeffreys*, Ann. Mag. Nat. Hist. 1856, vol. xviii. pl. 2, fig. 16.—Port Elizabeth (Crawford). Very rare in the Mediterranean.

APLYSIA MACULATA, *Rang*, Hist. Nat. des Aplys. p. 58, pl. 12, figs. 6–9.—Table Bay (Rang), Natal coast (Wahlberg). Port Elizabeth (Crawford). This is the shell quoted by me in the 'Journal of Conchology,' vol. vi. p. 13, as *Aplysia punctata*.

APLYSIA CONCAVA, *Sowerby*, Reeve, Conch. Icon. Aplysia, sp. 24.—Port Elizabeth.

APLYSIA SAVIGNYANA, *Férussac*, Rang, Hist. Nat. des Aplys. p. 69, pl. 20.—Natal coast (Krauss).

DOLABELLA RUMPHII, *Cuvier*, Ann. du Mus. vol. v. p. 437, pl. 29, fig. 1.—Natal Bay (Krauss).

PLEUROBRANCHUS GRANULATUS, *Krauss*, Sudafr. Moll. 61.

UMBRELLA INDICA. *Lamarck.*—A common species of wide distribution, but rarely found on the South African coast.

SIPHONARIA ASPERA, *Krauss*, Sudafr. Moll. p. 60, pl. 4. fig. 5.—Natal. Cape, and Port Elizabeth (abundant).

SIPHONARIA CAPENSIS, *Quoy et Gaim.*, Voy. de l'Astrol. vol. ii. p. 331, pl. 25, figs. 28. 29.—Port Elizabeth. &c.

(common). Var. *lineolata*, Krauss. Sudafr. Moll. p. 58, pl. 4. fig. 2.—Table Bay (Krauss). = *S. venosa*, Reeve.

SIPHONARIA OCULUS. *Krauss*, Sudafr. Moll. p. 58, pl. 4, fig. 3.—Table Bay (Krauss).

SIPHONARIA VARIABILIS. *Krauss*, Sudafr. Moll. p. 59, pl. 4. fig. 4a. Var. *S. concinna*, Sowb. Genera of Shells, fig. 2. Var. *albofasciata*. Krauss. Sudafr. Moll. p. 60. pl. 4, fig. 4b.

SIPHONARIA NATALENSIS. *Krauss*, Sudafr. Moll. p. 61, pl. 4, fig. 6.—Port Elizabeth. Table Bay. Simon's Bay, &c.

PELECYPODA.

PHOLAS DACTYLUS, *Linn.*—A somewhat stout form of this well-known British species found at Port Elizabeth.

MARTESIA FALCATA, *Gray*, Reeve, Conch. Icon. (Pholas), sp. 51.—Port Elizabeth.

TEREDO (HYPEROTUS) GREGATA, *Lamarck* (Fistulana) = *nucivora* (Spengler), Sowb. Thes. Conch. vol. v. pl. 469, fig. 16.—Ceylon, &c., as well as South Africa.

SILIQUA JAPONICA, *Dunker*. Reeve, Conch. Icon. Cultellus, sp. 15. Port Elizabeth. This species, known as Japanese, has also been found by Dr. Jousseaume at Aden.

SOLEN MARGINATUS, *Pulteney*, Sowb. Illust. Index Brit. Shells, pl. 2, fig. 14.—This common British species, also quoted by Krauss as South African, has been found at Port Elizabeth. This is possibly the *Solen vagina* (Linn.).

SOLEN REGULARIS, *Dunker*, Reeve, Conch. Icon. Solen, sp. 30.—Port Elizabeth.

SOLEN GOULDI. *Conrad*. Bost. Soc. Nat. Hist. 1862, vol. viii. p. 26.—Port Elizabeth.

CULTELLUS PELLUCIDUS. *Pennant* (Solen), Sowb. Illust. Index Brit. Shells, pl. 2, fig. 12.—Several perfect specimens of this well-known European species have been taken at Port Elizabeth.

CERATISOLEN LEGUMEN, *Linn.* (Solen), Sowb. Illust. Index Brit. Shells, pl. 2, fig. 11. Another common British species, of which several specimens have been found at Port Elizabeth.

SAXICAVA ARCTICA, *Linn.*, Sowb. Illust. Index Brit. Shells, pl. 1, fig. 16.—A specimen with serrated angle, exactly like the typical British form, found by Mr. Crawford at Port Elizabeth.

SAXICAVA AUSTRALIS, *Lamarck.*—The specimens shown me from South Africa look very much like the British *N. rugosa.*

CORBULA TUNICATA, *Hinds.* Zoo. Voy. Sulphur, Moll. p. 68, pl. 10, figs. 4, 5.—Agulhas Bank. Common in the China Sea, &c.

CORBULA CUNEATA, *Hinds.* Zoo. Voy. Sulphur, Moll. p. 68, pl. 10, fig. 6.—Like the last species this is not uncommon in the China Sea. It is quoted by Hinds from Agulhas Bank.

CUSPIDARIA CAPENSIS, *Smith.* Report Lamell. Challenger, p. 45, pl. 9, figs. 5-5b.—Off Cape of Good Hope.

THRACIA CAPENSIS, *Sowerby.* Journ. of Conch. vol. vi. 1889, p. 156, pl. 3, fig. 4.—Port Elizabeth.

THRACIA VILLOSIUSCULA, *Macgillivray.* Sowerby, Illust. Index Brit. Shells, pl. 2, fig. 9.—Port Elizabeth.

MACTRA ADANSONI, *Philippi*, Reeve, Conch. Icon. sp. 49. —A variable species, including *M. semistriata* (Deshayes) and probably *M. decora* (Deshayes).—Port Elizabeth. Senegal, Red Sea, &c.

MACTRA POLITA, *Chemnitz*, Reeve, Conch. Icon. sp. 39.— Cape, and Natal coast (Krauss).

MACTRA CAPENSIS, *Sowerby.* n. sp., pl. 3, fig. 68.—Testa elliptica, subæquilateralis, compressiuscula, albida, nitida, lævigata, concentrice subtilissime striata; umbones acutiusculi, elevati, approximati; margo dorsalis utrinque declivis, posticus obscure unicarinatus, ventralis mediocriter arcuatus.

Diam. antero-post 39, umbone marg. 29 mill.

Hab. Port Elizabeth (Crawford).

Somewhat resembling a white variety of *M. stultorum.*

but of a more transversely oval form, and with a slight keel at the posterior angle.

MACTRA (SCHIZODESMA) SPENGLERI. *Gmelin*, Reeve, Conch. Icon. (Mactra), sp. 27.—Cape of Good Hope.

LUTRARIA OBLONGA. *Chemnitz*, Sowerby. Illust. Index Brit. Shells, pl. 4, fig. 3. See note, Journ. of Conch. vol. vi. p. 155.—Port Elizabeth.

LUTRARIA INTERMEDIA, *Sowerby*, Illust. Index of Brit. Shells, pl. 4, fig. 2, as *L. elliptica* var.—Port Elizabeth.

LUTRARIA CAPENSIS. *Deshayes*, Reeve, Conch. Icon. pl. 3, fig. 9. See note, Journ. of Conch. vol. vi. p. 156.

STANDELLA SOLANDRI. *Gray*. Reeve, Conch. Icon. (Mactra), sp. 113.—Cape of Good Hope.

PSAMMOBIA VESPERTINA. *Gmelin*. Sowerby. Illust. Index of Brit. Shells, pl. 3, fig. 4.—Port Elizabeth.

PSAMMOTELLINA CAPENSIS, *Sowerby*. pl. 2, fig. 57; Journ. of Conch. 1889, vol. vi, p. 13, pl. 1, fig. 19. Port Elizabeth.

PSAMMOTELLA ROSEA, *Gmelin* (= *P. Ruppelliana*, Reeve), Conch. Icon. sp. 4.— Natal.

TELLINA PRISTIS, *Lamarck*, Sowerby, Thes. Conch. pl. 61, fig. 160. Natal coast (Wahlberg).

TELLINA FABULA, *Gmelin*, Sowerby, Illust. Index of Brit. Shells, pl. 3, fig. 16.—Natal Bay (Krauss).

TELLINA TENUIS, *Da Costa*, Sowerby, Illust. Index of Brit. Shells, pl. 3, figs. 12, 13.—Port Elizabeth.

TELLINA TRIANGULARIS, *Chemnitz*. Sowerby, Thes. Conch. vol. i. pl. 60, fig. 150.—Cape of Good Hope.

TELLINA CAPSOIDES, *Lamarck*, Sowerby, Thes. Conch. vol. i. pl. 62, fig. 185.—Natal coast. A common species in the East Indian Archipelago.

TELLINA PONSONBYI, *Sowerby*, pl. 2, fig. 58; Journ. of Conch. vol. vi. p. 155, pl. 3, fig. 1. –Port Elizabeth.

TELLINA NATALENSIS, *Krauss*, Sudafr. Moll. p. 3.—-Natal coast (Krauss).

TELLINA UMBONELLA, *Lamarck*, Sowerby, Thes. Conch. vol. i. pl. 56, fig. 13.--Cape of Good Hope.

TELLINA LUDWIGI, *Krauss*, Sudafr. Moll. p. 3, pl. 1, fig. 2.—Shores of Natal (Krauss).

TELLINA LITTORALIS, *Krauss*, Sudafr. Moll. p. 4, pl. 1, fig. 3.—Natal and Cape coast (Krauss).

TELLINA ORBICULARIS, *Sowerby*, pl. 3, fig. 64; Journ. of Conch. vol. vi. p. 13, pl. 1, fig. 20.--Port Elizabeth.

TELLINA ROSEA, *Spengler*, Sowerby, Thes. Conch. vol. i. pl. 61, fig. 170.--Common at Port Elizabeth.

TELLINA (MACOMA) CALCAREA, *Chemnitz*, Sowerby's Illust. Index of Brit. Shells, pl. 3, fig. 9.--Port Elizabeth.

TELLINA (MACOMA) CRAWFORDI, *Sowerby*, n. sp., pl. 3, fig. 71.—Testa suboblique-ovalis, æquivalvis, tennis, leviter compressa, snblævis, pallida; postice subtruncata, antice leviter producta. Umbones acuti, prominentes, conjuncti. Lunula leviter impressa. Margo dorsalis utrinque declivis; anticus elongatus, levissime arcuatus; posticus brevis, rectiusculus. Latus anticum rotundatum; posticum obtuse biangulatum. Cardo pertennis.

Diam. antero-post 25, umbono marg. 18 millim.

Hab. Port Elizabeth (Crawford).

A species of very ordinary form and character, allied to *T. cumana*, *T. lucerna*, &c., but distinguished principally by its remarkably thin hinge-line.

TELLINA (MACOMA) ROUSI, *Sowerby*, n. sp., pl. 3, fig. 70. - Testa oblongo-ovalis, æquivalvis, albida, tenninscula, parum inflata, lævinscula, concentrice striata; antice rotundata, postice leviter acuminata, umbones acutiusculi, paululum elevati, conjuncti, fere centrali. Cardo normalis.

Diam. antero-post 35, umbono marg. 25 millim.

Hab. Port Elizabeth.

Another species of very ordinary type, somewhat resembling *T. nasuta* (Conrad), but smaller and less acuminated posteriorly.

TELLINA (MACOMA) CUMANA, *Hanley*. Thes. Conch. vol. i. pl. 58, fig. 73. Port Elizabeth, Mediterranean, &c.

GASTRANA ABILGAARDIANA, *Spengler* = *G. Guinaica* (Chemnitz), Conch. Cab. vol. x. p. 170, figs. 1651-1653.—Port Elizabeth.

DONAX SERRA, *Chemnitz*, Sowb. Thes. Conch. vol. iii. pl. 282, fig. 87.—Common at Port Elizabeth.

DONAX SORDIDUS, *Reeve*, Conch. Icon. (Donax), pl. 5, fig. 32.—Cape (Krauss), Port Elizabeth.

DONAX ELONGATUS, *Lamarck*, Sowerby, Thes. Conch. vol. iii. pl. 280, fig. 12.—Port Elizabeth.

DONAX EXARATUS, *Krauss*, Sudafr. Mol. p. 6, pl. 1, fig. 5. —Natal (Krauss), Port Elizabeth (rare).

DONAX SEMISULCATUS, *Hanley*, Conch. Icon. (Donax), pl. 4, fig. 25.—Indian Ocean, Port Elizabeth (rare).

DONAX OWENI, *Gray*, Sowb., Thes. Conch. vol. iii. pl. 1, fig. 8.—Port Elizabeth (rare).

DONAX BIPARTITUS, *Sowerby*, nov. sp., pl. 3, fig. 74.— Testa subtrigono-oblonga, valde inaequilateralis, solidiuscula, mediocriter compressa, albida, obscure pallide violaceo radiata, antice laevigata, nitens, postice transversim crenato lirata, obscurissime radiatim sulcata; umbones acuti, prominentes. Lunula leviter impressa; margo dorsalis anticus elongatus, leviter declivis, posticus abrupte truncatus; area postica dense clathrata; pagina interna albida, antice obscure violaceo radiatim tincta, postice nigro-purpureo uniradiata; cardo normalis.

Diam. antero-post 20, umbono marg. 11 millim.

This species, of which Mr. Ponsonby has shown me several specimens, may be distinguished by the intense violet ray inside the posterior end. Rather less than half the valve is sculptured, and the remaining portion smooth and polished.

CYTHEREA (TIVELA) COMPRESSA, *Sowerby*, Thes. Conch. vol. ii. pl. 128, figs. 33, 34.—Large, well-grown specimens of this species from Port Elizabeth I at first thought distinct, but upon further comparison am unable to separate them. *C. polita* (Sowerby) is merely the young of this species.

CYTHEREA (TIVELA) DOLABELLA, *Sowerby*, Thes. Conch. vol. ii. pl. 127, fig. 15.—Port Elizabeth.

CYTHEREA (CALLISTA) HEBRÆA, *Sowerby*, Thes. Conch. vol. ii. pl. 13, figs. 143-148.—Natal.

CIRCE (CRISTA) PECTINATA, *Linn.*, Sowerby, Thes. Conch. vol. ii. pl. 137, figs. 1-3 = *Cytherea Savignyi* (Jonas).—Red Sea, Natal coast (Krauss). Port Elizabeth (Crawford). Also found in various parts of the Indian Ocean.

MEROË OVALIS, *Sowerby*, nov. sp., pl. 3, fig. 69. —Testa ovalis, æquivalvis, crassa, leviter compressa, lævis, pallide carnea, lineis pallidis violaceis angulatis, et concentricis sparsim picta. Umbones obtusi, haud prominentes. Area ligamenti profundissima. Cardo normalis. Pagina interna carnea.
Diam. antero-post 22, umbono-marg. 15 millim.
Hab. Port Elizabeth.
Mr. Ponsonby has shown me a single valve, much worn, and quite colourless, of a much larger specimen, measuring 35 × 25 millim. The smaller specimen, which I have taken for the type, has a few faint markings like those of *S. scripta*. The general character of the shell is more like *S. menstrualis*, or *excavata*, but of a more oblong-oval form.

TAPES CORRUGATUS, *Deshayes*, Sowerby, Thes. Conch. vol. ii. pl. 150, figs. 121-122.—Common at Port Elizabeth.

TAPES RUGOSUS, *Deshayes*, is *Venerupis rugosa*.

TAPES TEXTRIX, *Chemnitz*, Conch. Icon. (Tapes), pl. 2, fig. 3.

TAPES PAUPERCULUS, *Chemnitz*, is *T. Kochi*.

TAPES DESHAYESII, *Hanley*, Thes. Conch. vol. ii. pl. 146, figs. 35-38.—Port Elizabeth.

TAPES PULLASTRA, *Montagu* (Venus), Sowb., Illust. Index Brit. Shells, pl. 4, fig. 4.—This common British species is quoted by Krauss, on the authority of Wahlberg and Zeyher, from Natal and Algoa Bay.

TAPES DACTYLOIDES, *Sowerby*, Thes. Conch. vol. ii. pl. 158, fig. 129.—Port Elizabeth (rare).

TAPES GEOGRAPHICUS, *Linn.*, Sowerby, Thes. Conch. vol. ii. pl. 149, fig. 90.—A well-known Mediterranean species, quoted by Krauss from Natal Bay.

TAPES CUMINGII, *Sowerby*, Thes. Conch. vol. ii. pl. 150, fig. 128.—South Africa?

TAPES KRAUSSII, *Deshayes*, Reeve, Conch. Icon. (Tapes), pl. 9, fig. 41.—Natal.

TAPES (HEMITAPES) AFRICANUS, *Muhlfeldt* (Venus), Thes. Conch. vol. ii. pl.159, fig. 159.—Cape (Philippi).

TAPES (HEMITAPES) KOCHII, *Philippi*, Sowb. Thes. Conch. (Venus), vol. ii. pl. 158, figs. 147–151.

VENUS (CHIONE) VERRUCOSA, *Linn.*—Natal Bay (Krauss), Port Elizabeth.   The South African variety of this common European species, quoted by me as var.*capensis* in the Journal of Conch. vol. vi. p. 14, may be readily distinguished.

VENUS (CHIONE) LAYARDI, *Reeve*, Conch. Icon. (Venus), pl. 26, fig. 126.—Port Elizabeth.

VENUS (GOMPHINA) UNDULOSA, *Lamarck*, Sowb. Thes. Conch. vol. ii. pl. 158, fig. 142.—Port Elizabeth (rare).   A common Australian species.

DOSINIA LINCTA, *Pulteney*, Sowb. Illust. Index of Brit. Shells, pl. 4, fig. 11.—Quoted by me in the 'Journal of Conchology,' vol. vi. p. 157, as *Dosinia cretacea* (Reeve). Several specimens I have seen from Port Elizabeth are unquestionably the same as the British species.   *D. africana* (Gray) is a variety of the same.

DOSINIA LAMELLATA, *Reeve*, Conch. Icon. (Artemis), pl. 3, fig. 13.—Port Elizabeth.

DOSINIA HEPATICA, *Lamarck*, Reeve, Conch. Icon. pl. 1, fig. 7.—*A. consobrina* (Deshayes) is a variety of this species.—Port Elizabeth.

VENERUPIS CORDIERI, *Deshayes*, Sowerby, Thes. Conch. vol. ii. pl. 164, fig. 2.—Port Elizabeth.

VENERUPIS RUGOSA, *Deshayes*, Sowerby, Thes. Conch. vol. ii. pl. 165, fig. 25.— Port Elizabeth.

PETRICOLA TYPICA, *Jonas*, Sowerby, Thes. Conch. vol. ii. pl. 166, fig. 21.—Port Elizabeth.

PETRICOLA ROBUSTA, *Sowerby*, Thes. Conch. vol. ii. pl. 166, fig. 16.—Port Elizabeth.

PETRICOLA CULTELLUS, *Deshayes*, Sowerby, Thes. Conch. vol. ii. pl. 166, fig. 5.—Port Elizabeth, Ceylon, &c. This species is nearly allied to the American *P. pholadiformis*.

PETRICOLA VENTRICOSA, *Krauss*, Sudafr. Moll. p. 2, pl. 1, fig. 1.—Natal coast (Krauss).

PETRICOLA PONSONBYI, *Sowerby*, nov. sp., pl. 3, fig. 68.— Testa ovata, compressinscula, solidula, albida, striis numerosis subrugosis divergentibus radiatim sculpta; umbones obtusi, vix prominentes; cardo normalis; pagina interna albida.

Diam. antero-post 20, umbono-marg. 15 mill.

Hab. Port Elizabeth.

An oval species with divaricating sculpture.

CARDIUM NATALENSE, *Krauss*, Sudafr. Moll. p. 12, pl. 1, fig. 9.—Natal (Krauss), Port Elizabeth.

CARDIUM (PAPYRIDEA) SEMISULCATUM, *Gray* = *C. ringiculum*, Sowerby, Reeve, Conch. Icon. (Cardium), pl. 21, f. 115; Smith, Report of the Lamellibranchiata of the 'Challenger,' p. 162.—Simon's Bay, 15-20 fath.

CARDIUM LIMA, *Gmelin* = *C. asiaticum* (Brug.). Reeve, Conch. Icon. (Cardium), pl. 18, fig. 90.—Natal (Krauss), Port Elizabeth. Nicobar Islands, &c.

CARDIUM FASCIATUM, *Montagu*. Sowb. Illust. Index Brit. Shells, pl. 5, fig. 7.—Port Elizabeth (large valves).

CHAMA GRYPHOIDES, *Linn.*—Natal.

LUCINA COLUMBELLA, *Lamarck*, Reeve, Conch. Icon. (Lucina), pl. 6, fig. 30. -Port Elizabeth.

LUCINA (DIVARICELLA) LIRATULA, *Sowerby*, pl. 2, fig. 63; Journ. of Conch. vol. vi. p. 155, pl. 3, fig. 5.—Port Elizabeth.

LORIPES LACTEUS, *Linn.* = *Lucina lactea*, Sowb. Illust. Index of Brit. Shells, pl. 5, fig. 17. = *Lucina leucoma* (Turton) = *L. fragilis* (Philippi).—Port Elizabeth.

LORIPES GLOBOSUS, *Forskael*, pl. 4, fig. 91; Descrip. Anim. in Itin. Observ. p. 53.—Port Elizabeth.

FELANIA SUBRADIATA, *Sowerby*, n. sp., pl. 3, fig. 73.—
Testa suborbicularis. tenuiuscula, complanata, fere æqui-
lateralis, luteo-albida, epidermide tenui luteo-fusca nitida
induta, concentrice irregulariter striata. Umbones prominentes, acutiusculi, approximati; margo dorsalis utrinque
declivis. Pagina interna albida, obscure rufo-radiata.

Diam. antero-post 19, umbono-marg. 20 millim.

Hab. Port Elizabeth.

I have described this from a single valve, but have since
seen a perfect specimen of smaller size in which the
internal pink rays are scarcely visible.

LASEA AUSTRALIS, *Souverbie*, Journ. de Conch. 1863,
pl. 12, fig. 8.—Port Elizabeth.

LASEA SEMINULUM, *Philippi* (Bornea), Moll. Sicil. vol. i.
p. 14, pl. 1, fig. 16; Krauss, Sudafr. Moll. p. 2.

KELLIA MACTROIDES, *Hanley*, pl. 4, fig. 92; Proc. Zool.
Soc. 1856, p. 341 (as *Pythina*).—Port Elizabeth.

KELLIA ROTUNDA, *Deshayes*, pl. 4. fig. 93; Proc. Zool.
Soc. 1855, p. 181 (as Erycina).—Port Elizabeth.

KELLIA SUBORBICULARIS, *Montagu*, Sowb. Illust. Index
Brit. Shells, pl. 6. fig. 5.—Port Elizabeth.

MONTACUTA CAPENSIS. *Sowerby*, pl. 2, fig. 62; Journ. of
Conch. vol. vi. p. 157, pl. 3, fig. 8. —Port Elizabeth.

CRASSATELLA ACUMINATA, *Sowerby*, pl. 2, fig. 59; Journ.
of Conch. vol. vi. p. 156, pl. 3. fig. 6.—Port Elizabeth.

CRASSATELLA SUBQUADRATA, *Sowerby*, Proc. Zool. Soc.
1870, p. 249.—Agulhas Bank.

CRASSATELLA CREBRELIRATA, *Sowerby*, Proc. Zool. Soc.
1870, p. 249.—Agulhas Bank.

CARDITA (MYTILICARDIA) VARIEGATA, *Bruguière*, Reeve,
Conch. Icon. (Cardita), pl. 1, fig. 3.—Natal (Krauss). This
species is found in many localities, from the Red Sea to
China, and from South Africa to Australia.

CARDITA (THECALIA) CONCAMERATA, *Bruguière*, Reeve,
Conch. Icon. (Cardita), pl. 9, fig. 42.—Port Elizabeth, Natal,
Table Bay, &c.

CARDITA ELATA, *Sowerby*, n. sp., pl. 3, fig. 67.—Testa parva, elata, subtrigona, crassiuscula, alba, concentrice sulcata, costis 16–17, subangulatis, leviter crenatis. Umbones prominentes, incurvi. Lunula parva, excavata. Margo dorsalis posticus valde declivis. Cardo normalis. Pagina interna alba, margine crenato.

Diam. antero-post 4, umbono-marg. 5 millim.

Hab. Port Elizabeth.

A curious little species, somewhat the form of an Isocardia. I have at present only seen odd valves.

CARDITELLA CAPENSIS, *Smith*, Report Lambellib. Voy. Challenger, p. 216. For description of the genus see Proc. Zool. Soc. 1881, p. 42.—Simon's Bay.

CARDITELLA RUGOSA, *Sowerby*, n. sp., pl. 3, fig. 65.— Testa parva, trapeziformis, albida, fusco sparsim maculata, radiatim costata, costis circ. 16, rugosis, interstitiis profundis. Umbones vix elevati, obtusi, approximati. Lunula elongata, impressa. Pagina interna fusca, margine fimbriato.

Diam. antero-post 6, umbono-marg. 4½ millim.

A little, roughly ribbed, trapeziform species.

NEOCARDIA, *Sowerby*, gen. nov.—Testa æquivalvis, valde inæquilateralis, extus cancellata, cardine angusto, obsolete bidentatc dente laterali postico elongato duplicato, margine antico edentulo.

NEOCARDIA ANGULATA, *Sowerby*, n. sp., pl. 3, fig. 66.— Testa parva, sub-mytiliformis, postice angulata, antice rotundata, albida, fusco-tincta, concentrice dense regulariter et profunde sulcata, radiatim costata, costis circ. 12 angustis, parum elevatis, leviter nodulosis. Umbones prominentes, acuti. Pagina interna obscure radiatim sulcata, plus minusve fusco-tincta.

Diam. antero-post 4¼, umbono-marg. 4 millim.

Hab. Port Elizabeth.

A remarkable little shell of distinct form and peculiarly cancellated sculpture. The cardinal teeth are scarcely visible, and there is only one elongated lateral tooth, which is on the posterior side of the hinge, the anterior being plain.

MYTILUS CRENATUS, *Lamarck*, Encyclo. Method. pl. 217, fig. 3; Sowerby's Genera of Shells, fig. 5. = *M. capensis* (Dunker).—Port Elizabeth.

MYTILUS PERNA, *Linn.*, Reeve, Conch. Icon. (Mytilus), pl. 6, fig. 23.—Port Elizabeth, &c.

MYTILUS EDULIS, *Linn.*, var. *M. meridionalis*, Krauss, Sudafr. Moll. p. 21, pl. 11. fig. 7.—Port Elizabeth, &c.

MYTILUS AFER, *Gmelin*, Reeve, Conch. Icon. (Mytilus), pl. 2, fig. 3.—Characterised by more or less pronounced brown zigzag markings; it is, however, extremely doubtful whether this is rightly considered a species distinct from *M. perna*.

MYTILUS VARIABILIS, *Krauss*, Sudafr. Moll. p. 25, pl. 2, fig. 3.—Table Bay. Natal and Port Elizabeth.

MYTILUS MAGELLANICUS, *Chemnitz*, Reeve, Conch. Icon. sp. 22.—A young specimen of this species found on the shore at Natal.

MODIOLA CAPENSIS, *Krauss*, Sudafr. Moll. p. 20, pl. 2, fig. 3.—Knysna River (Krauss).

MODIOLA AURICULATA, *Krauss*, Sudafr. Moll, pl. 2. fig. 4. — Natal (Krauss), Port Elizabeth (Bairstow), I. Anjonan (Philippi), Red Sea (Rüppell).

MODIOLA CYLINDRICA, *Krauss*, Sudafr. Moll. p. 21, pl. 2, fig. 2.—Natal (Krauss).

MODIOLA MUCRONATA, *Philippi*, Abbild. und Beschr. neuer Conchyl., vol. ii. p. 150, pl. 1, fig. 8. Natal coast (Krauss).

MODIOLA LIGNEA, *Reeve*, Conch. Icon. (Modiola), pl. 10, fig. 58.— Port Elizabeth. An Australian species.

MODIOLA ELEGANS, *Philippi*. Reeve, Conch. Icon. sp. 19. Port Elizabeth. Much larger than the typical Indo-Pacific form.

MODIOLA PETAGNÆ, *Scacchi*, Reeve, Conch. Icon. (Modiola), pl. 8, fig. 46.—Port Elizabeth. A Mediterranean species.

MODIOLARIA CUNEATA, *Gould*, is *M. marmorata*.

MODIOLARIA DISCORS, *Linn.*, Sowb., Ill. Index of British Shells, pl. 7, fig. 13.—Port Elizabeth. A common British and European species.

MODIOLARIA MARMORATA, *Forbes*, Sowb. Illust. Index of British Shells, pl. 8, fig. 14.—Specimens from Port Elizabeth, hardly distinguishable from the European. This is no doubt the *M. cuneata* of Gould, said to be South African. *Vide* Smith in P. Z. S. 1891, p. 393.

AVICULA (MELEAGRINA) CAPENSIS, *Sowerby*, pl. 3, fig. 75; Journal of Conchology, 1889, vol. vi. p. 158, pl. 3, fig. 10. — Port Elizabeth.

PERNA DENTIFERA, *Krauss*, Sudafr. Moll. p. 28, pl. 11, fig. 9.—Natal (Krauss).

PERNA VULSELLA, *Lamarck*, Reeve, Conch. Icon. (Perna), pl. 5, fig. 21.—Natal (Krauss).

PINNA PERNULA, *Chemnitz*, Reeve, Conch. Icon. sp. 22. = *P. squamifera (Sowerby)*. — Mouth of river Knysna (Krauss), Port Elizabeth (Crawford).

ARCA ACUMINATA, *Krauss*, Sudafr. Moll. p. 14, pl. 1, fig. 11.—Natal (Krauss).

ARCA (BARBATIA) LACTEA, *Linn.*, Sowb. Illust. Index of Brit. Shells, pl. 8, fig. 8.—Port Elizabeth. A well-known British and European species.

ARCA IMBRICATA, *Brug.* = *A. Kraussi* (Philippi), Sudfr. Moll. p. 14, pl. 1, fig. 13. = *A. canealis* (Reeve) = *A. mutabilis* (Sowb.).—Natal.

ARCA (BARBATIA) SQUAMOSA, *Lamarck*, Hist. Anim. s. vert. ed. 2, vol. vi. p. 474.—Natal (Krauss), West Indies, Red Sea, &c.

ARCA (BARBATIA) NIVEA, *Chemnitz*, Reeve, Conch. Icon. sp. 96.—Natal (Krauss). Common in the Red Sea, &c.

ARCA (BARBATIA) OBLIQUATA, *Gray*, Reeve, Conch. Icon. sp. 80.—Natal (Krauss), Port Elizabeth.

ARCA (SCAPHARCA) NATALENSIS, *Krauss*, Sudafr. Moll. p. 17, pl. 1, fig. 12.—Natal (Krauss).

ARCA (BARBATIA) SCABRA, *Poli.*, Test. Utr. Sicil. vol. ii. pl. 25, fig. 22.—Port Elizabeth, Mediterranean, &c.

K

ARCA (SCAPHARCA) SCAPHA, *Chemnitz*, Reeve, Conch. Icon. sp. 25.—Port Elizabeth.

PECTUNCULUS ARABICUS, *H. Adams*, Proc. Zool. Soc. 1870, p. 792; Savigny's Descrip. Egypte, pl. x. fig. 4.

PECTUNCULUS INÆQUALIS, *Sowerby*, Reeve, Conch. Icon. sp. 16.—Table Bay (Krauss), Panama.

LIMOPSIS BELCHERI, *Adams & Reeve*, Voy. Samarang, Moll. p. 76, pl. 22, fig. 5.—Cape, 120 fath.

NUCULINA OVALIS, *Searles Wood*, Smith, Report Lamell. Challenger, p. 230.—Simon's Bay, 15-20 fath.

NUCULA RADIATA, *Forbes et Hanley*, Sowb. Illust. Index of British Shells, pl. 8, fig. 3.—Port Elizabeth.

NUCULA NUCLEUS, *Linn.*, Sowb. Illust. Index of British Shells, pl. 8, fig. 1.—Port Elizabeth.

NUCULA PULCHRA, *Hinds*, Zool. Voy. Sulphur, Moll. p. 62, pl. 18, fig. 3.—Agulhas Bank.

NUCULA BELCHERI, *Hinds*, Zool. Voy. Sulphur, Moll. p. 63, pl. 18, fig. 11.—Agulhas Bank (very rare).

PECTEN LIMATULA, *Reeve*, var., Smith, Report Lamellib. Challenger, p. 297.—South Africa.

PECTEN PUSIO, *Linn.* Several varieties.—Port Elizabeth, Natal (Krauss).

PECTEN (VOLA) CAPENSIS, *Gray*.—Port Elizabeth.

LIMA ROTUNDATA, *Sowerby*, Thes. Conch. vol. i. pl. 21, fig. 19.—Port Elizabeth.

LIMA MULTICOSTATA, *Sowerby*, Thes. Conch. vol. i. pl. 22, fig. 38.—A specimen in the Bairstow collection.

PLICATULA AUSTRALIS, *Lamarck*, Sowb. Thes. Conch. vol. i. pl. 91, fig. 21.—Natal (Krauss).

OSTREA PRISMATICA, *Gray*, Conch. Icon. pl. 1, fig. 1.— = *iridescens*, Gray.—Port Elizabeth.

OSTREA ALGOENSIS, *Sowerby*, Conch. Icon. (Ostrea), pl. 26, fig. 65.—Port Elizabeth.

OSTREA RUFA, *Lamarck* = *O. australis* (Lamk.) = *tuber-culata* (Lamk.), Conch. Icon. (Ostrea), sp. 25.—Algoa Bay, and Natal coast (Krauss).

OSTREA CUCULLATA, *Born*, Conch. Icon. pl. 16, fig. 34. Natal coast (Krauss). Found on various coasts in the Indian and Pacific Oceans.

OSTREA ROSACEA, *Chemnitz*, Conch. Icon. sp. 46.- Natal coast (Krauss).

BRACHIOPODA.

TEREBRATULINA RADIATA, *Reeve*, Conch. Icon. (Terebra-tula) sp. 7 ?=*abyssicola* (Ad. & Rve.).—Port Elizabeth.

KRAUSSIA RUBRA, *Pallas*=*Terebratula capensis*, Krauss, Sudafr. Moll. p. 32, pl. 2, fig. 10.—Port Elizabeth.

KRAUSSIA COGNATA, *Chemnitz* (Anomia), Reeve, Conch. Icon. (Terebratula), sp. 38.—It is doubtful whether this is distinct from *K. rubra.* I have not met with it among South African shells.

KRAUSSIA NATALENSIS, *Krauss* (Terebratula), Sudafr. Moll. p. 33, pl. 2, fig. 11.—Natal.

KRAUSSIA PISUM, *Valenciennes* (Terebratula), Reeve, Conch. Icon. (Terebratula), sp. 36.—Port Elizabeth and Natal.

KRAUSSIA DESHAYESII, *Davidson*, Reeve, Conch. Icon. (Terebratula). pl. 9, fig. 35.

ADDENDUM.

GIBBULA BIPORCATA, *Sowerby* (A. Adams, MSS. p. 44). Testa orbiculata, subcompressa, solidiuscula, perforata, carneo-albida, roseo strigata vel maculata; spira abbreviato-conica, gradata ; anfractus 4, angulati, spiraliter striati ; anfr. ultimus valde bicarinatus ; basis planato-convexa, spiraliter striata ; apertura lata, obliqua; peristoma tenue, margine columellari sursum tenuiter dilatato, perforationem fere tegente.

Diam. 6, alt. 5 millim.

Hab. Cape Town (Cuming).

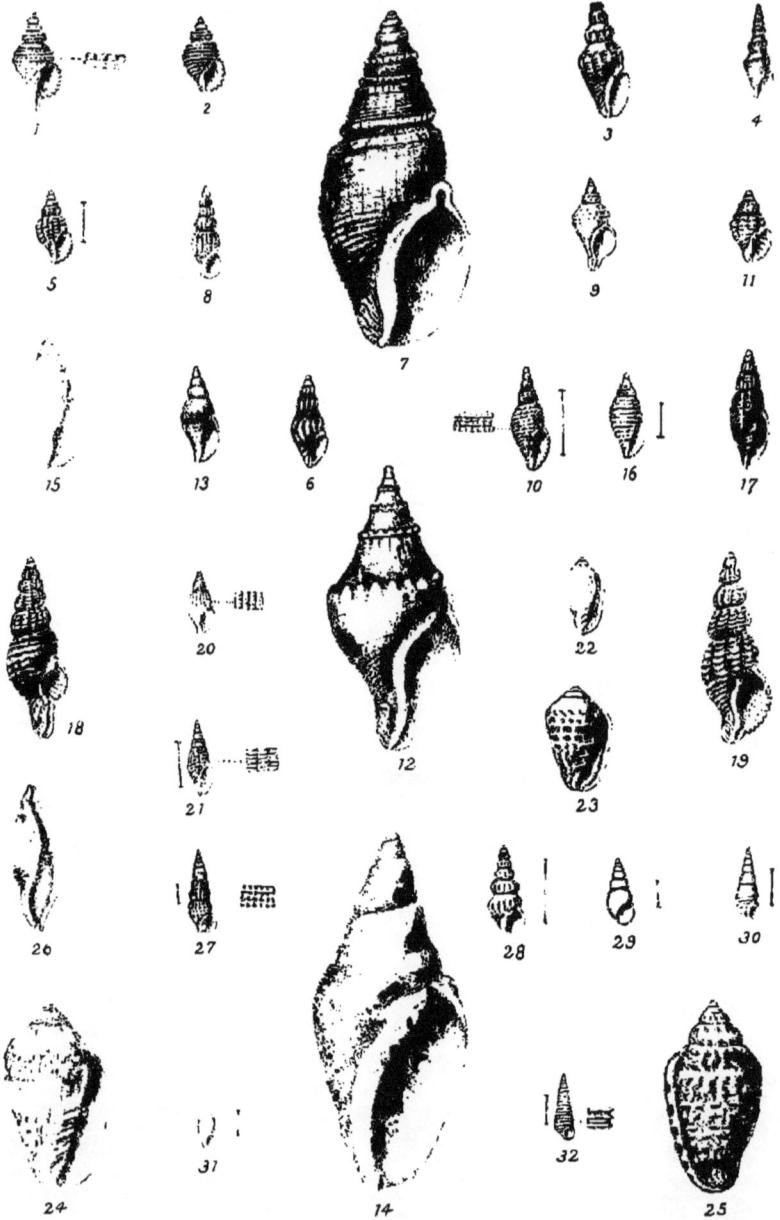

DESCRIPTION OF PLATE I.

Fig. 1. Murex Babingtoni, p. 2.
„ 2. „ Crawfordi, p. 2.
„ 3. Pleurotoma Rousi, p. 5.
„ 4. „ Wilkiæ, p. 4.
„ 5. Defrancia Ponsonbyi, p. 7.
„ 6. Pleurotoma Bairstowi, p. 6.
„ 7. Cominella semisulcata, p. 10.
„ 8. „ angusta, p. 10.
„ 9. „ puncturata, p. 11.
„ 10. „ sulcata, p. 11.
„ 11. „ unifasciata, p 11.
„ 12. Euthria Ponsonbyi, p. 4.
13. „ fusco-tincta, p. 4.
„ 14. Pseudoliva ancilla, p. 15.
„ 15. Ancilla pura, p. 17.
„ 16. Mitromorpha volva, p. 7.
„ 17. Mitra merula, p. 19.
„ 18. Latirus Bairstowi, p. 17.
„ 19. „ Rousi, p. 17.
„ 20. Columbella capensis, p. 22.
„ 21. „ algoensis, p. 22.
„ 22. Marginella electrina, p. 21.
„ 23. „ Bairstowi, p. 19.
„ 24. „ lineolata, p. 19.
„ 25. „ floccata, p. 20.
26. Ovula aurantia, p. 34.
„ 27. Cerithium foveolatum, p. 36.
„ 28. Diala capensis, p. 27.
„ 29. „ dubia, p. 27.
30. „ infrasulcata, p. 27.
31. Eulima Langleyi, p. 27.
„ 32. Cingulina acutilirata, p. 27.

DESCRIPTION OF PLATE II.

Plate 3

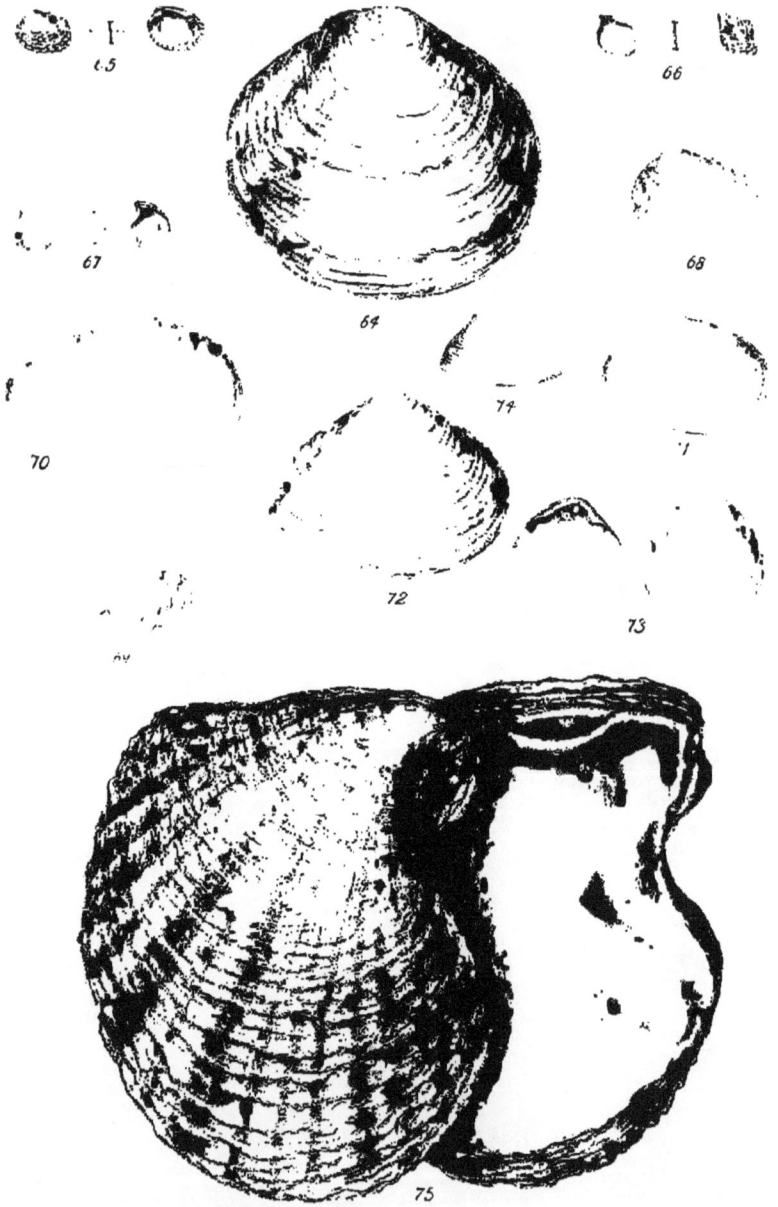

G B Sowerby lith.

Hanhart imp

DESCRIPTION OF PLATE III.

L.

76

92

93

77

78

79

80

84

86

81

85

90

88

82

81

83

91

89

G.B.Sowerby lith.

Hanhart imp

DESCRIPTION OF PLATE IV.

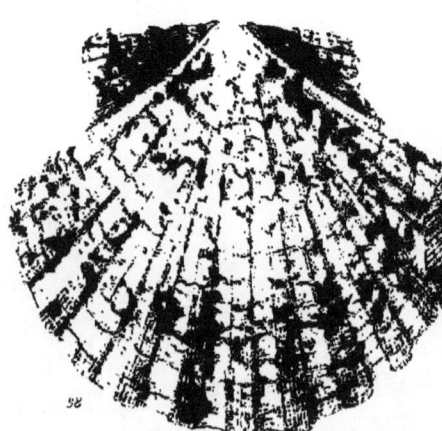

DESCRIPTION OF PLATE V.

INDEX

M

ERRATUM.

P. 66. For *Pecten capensis*, Gray, read PECTEN (VOLA) SULCICOSTATUS, *Sowerby*, pl. 5, figs. 97, 98, *Thes. Conch.*, vol. i. p. 7, pl. xiii. figs. 35, 36 ; Dunker, *Novitates Conch.*, ' Meeres Conchylien,' p. 67, pl. xxiii. figs. 4–6 = *Pecten capensis*, Gray (mss. in Brit. Mus.). Hab. : Natal coast (Dunker), Cape of Good Hope (Brit. Mus), Port Elizabeth. The shell figured plate v. has been in the British Museum since 1837, named *P. capensis*, Gray, but it does not appear that any description of it has ever been published under that name. The specimen is very much larger than the original type, but I have no doubt as to its identity.